THE IMPOSSIBLE LAND

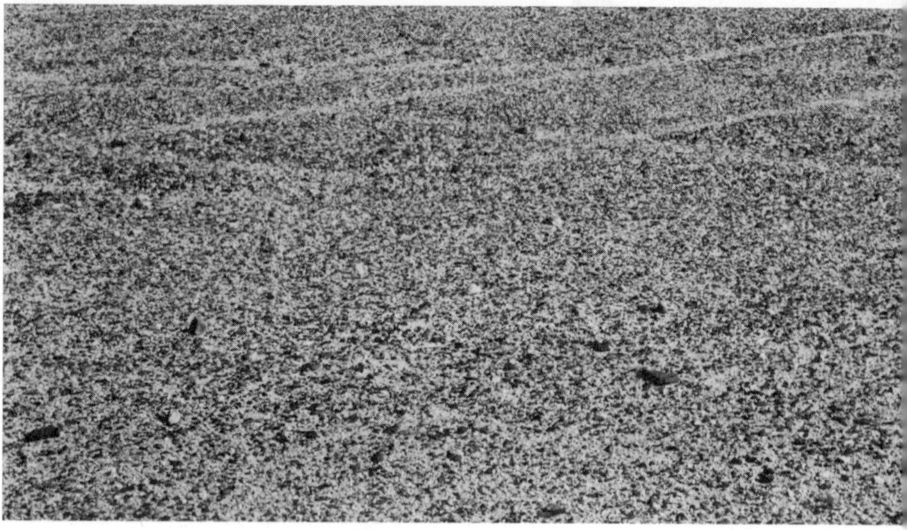

The Impossible Land

STORY AND PLACE IN CALIFORNIA'S IMPERIAL VALLEY

PHILLIP H. ROUND

UNIVERSITY OF NEW MEXICO PRESS | ALBUQUERQUE

FOR EVERYBODY
(especially you)

© 2008 by Phillip H. Round
All rights reserved. Published 2008
Printed in the United States of America
15 14 13 12 11 10 09 08   1 2 3 4 5 6 7 8

LIBRARY OF CONGRESS CATALOGING-IN-PUBLICATION DATA
Round, Phillip H., 1958–
The impossible land : story and place in California's
    Imperial Valley / Phillip H. Round.
        p. cm.
    Includes bibliographical references and index.
        ISBN 978-0-8263-4323-9 (PBK. : ALK. PAPER)
1. Imperial Valley (Calif. and Mexico)—In literature.
2. Imperial Valley (Calif. and Mexico)—History.
3. Imperial Valley (Calif. and Mexico)—Social conditions.
4. Regionalism—Imperial Valley (Calif. and Mexico)
5. Regionalism—In literature.
6. Group identity—Imperial Valley (Calif. and Mexico)
I. Title.
    F868.I2R68 2008
    979.4'99—dc22
                    2007046329

Book and cover design and type composition by Kathleen Sparkes.
This book was composed using Utopia OT STD 9.7/13; 26P.
    Display type is Berthold Akzindenz Grotesk.

The valley or desert as it was then dry
and bushy with plenty of sidewinders and
scorpions also plenty other bugs. The
ground was so hot part of the year we had
to run or jump from one bush to the shade
of another to keep from burning our feet,
but they were quite tough from going bare
foot most of the time. We were also well
and no one got snake bit because we knew
how to take care of ourselves. I am sure
the Lord was with us too.

    —Susie Van Horn Atkins,
    Imperial Valley Pioneer

CONTENTS

List of Illustrations   ix

Acknowledgments   xi

Introduction The Place of Storytelling   1

    1 The Impossible Land   19

    2 "Silence and Desolation"   33

    3 "Water is King, Here is its Kingdom"   51

    4 American Exodus   69

    5 "A Dying Reed by the River Bed"   105

    6 *Travesías*   129

    7 A Heart of Fire   151

Epilogue "Are there mandolins of western mountains?"   173

Bibliography   183

Index   189

LIST OF ILLUSTRATIONS

FIGURE 1. Leo Hetzel, *Imperial Valley Flood, 1926* 2
FIGURE 2. Satellite photograph of the Imperial Valley 20
FIGURE 3. Leo Hetzel, *Imperial Valley Plank Road* 26
FIGURE 4. O. V. Blackburn's map of Imperial County 29
FIGURE 5. *Silence and Desolation*, from *The Desert* (1901) 40
FIGURE 6. Emma Augusta Ayer, *Desolation on the Yuma Desert* 48
FIGURE 7. Leo Hetzel, *Lobby, Barbara Worth Hotel* 66
FIGURE 8. Dorothea Lange, *Migrant Mother* 78
FIGURE 9. Dorothea Lange, *Old Mexican Laborer Saying, "I Have Worked All My Life and All I Have Now Is My Broken Body"* 79
FIGURE 10. Dorothea Lange, *Mexican Girl Who Picks Peas for the Eastern Market* 80
FIGURE 11. Dorothea Lange, *One of the Roads Leading into Calipatria, Imperial County, California* 81
FIGURE 12. Dorothea Lange, *Capped Cantaloupe. Imperial Valley, California* 82
FIGURE 13. Dorothea Lange, *Irrigation Ditch along the Road. Imperial Valley, California* 86
FIGURE 14. Dorothea Lange, *Laguna Dam* 87
FIGURE 15. Dorothea Lange, *Desert Agriculture. Brushed Chili Field. Replanting Chili Plants on a Japanese-owned Ranch* 88
FIGURE 16. Dorothea Lange, *The Kind of Work Drought Refugees and Mexicans Do in the Imperial Valley, California* 89
FIGURE 17. Dorothea Lange, *Homes of Mexican Field Laborers. Brawley, Imperial Valley, California* 92
FIGURE 18. Dorothea Lange, *Drinking Water for Field Worker's Family* 94
FIGURE 19. Dorothea Lange, *Neideffer Camp, Holtville, Imperial Valley, California* 98
FIGURE 20. Dorothea Lange, *Refugee Families Encamped near Holtville, California* 100
FIGURE 21. Russell Lee, *Exhibit of Grapefruit at the Imperial County Fair, California* 102

| ix

FIGURE 22. Leo Hetzel, *Japanese Armistice Day, Imperial Valley, 1928* 114
FIGURE 23. Jack Matsuoka, *Greetings from the First Americans* 119
FIGURE 24. Fred Clark, *Jim Morikawa Sprinkling in an Attempt to Settle the Dust.* Poston Internment Camp, 1942 120
FIGURE 25. Leo Hetzel, *The Owl Café, Mexicali* 142
FIGURE 26. Mark Ruwedel, *Lake Cahuilla, Yuha Desert. The Yuha Geoglyph* 170
FIGURE 27. Mark Ruwedel, *Yuha Desert: Where the Ancient Trail Divides into Three* 174

ACKNOWLEDGMENTS

| First thanks go to the people of the Imperial Valley who shared their stories with me. In addition to the staff of the Imperial County Pioneers Museum, I would like to express my appreciation to many lifelong friends who hail from the valley: Jack and Dee Cato, Brian and Connie Stokely, Jim and Laurie Halfpenny, Mark and Kathy Kellogg, and Ray and Nancy Acevedo. They have given me much-needed support over the years. Among those valleyites who helped me during my research for this book, I want to extend a very special thanks to Henry and Albert Escalera, who introduced me to Ramón Becerra, and who always offered me welcome words of encouragement. Thanks also to Leonard Vasquez for sharing his cowboy bildungsroman, to Norma Sosa, who told me the story of *La Llorona*, and to Frank Meredith, who showed me the way to Everybody's Market. I owe a debt of gratitude as well to valley historian Benny Andres. His dissertation about labor relations in the Imperial County was invaluable in providing me with the latest research on that important

arena of the region's cultural formation. Finally, I would like to acknowledge the help of Sheila Dollente, who shared her perspective on living in the valley as a teacher and scholar.

Two colleagues at Iowa, Claire Fox and John Raeburn, also lent a hand by loaning me books and answering my questions about their areas of expertise. It was Claire who first introduced me to the works of Gabriel Muñoz Trujillo, and John who let me read a chapter from *A Staggering Revolution* before it appeared in print. Thanks go as well to the Office of the Vice President for Research at the University of Iowa, which provided a subvention for this book. I would also like to recognize the assistance of Drew Heath Johnson, curator of photography at the Oakland Museum, who directed me to Lange's field notes and guided me through the museum's extensive collective of her prints and negatives.

Finally, I would like to thank my family, who both asked for and then aided in the production of this book. My mother and father, Jay and Beverly Round, told me my first valley stories. Beverly's sister, Yvonne Smith, extended and elaborated on my parents' storytelling tradition. My sister, Daryl Hern, has kept me posted on events in the valley over the years, sending me clippings and moral support along the way. My wife, Teresa Lopes, has read every word of this book in its many incarnations, always pushing me to write with my readers in mind, encouraging me to share with them the great pleasure I've had in telling stories of the Lower Colorado. As a northern border dweller who came of age looking across the Detroit River to an impossible land on the American side, she had no idea that she would someday become a part of the Imperial Valley's history and its stories. I'm glad she did.

INTRODUCTION
The Place of Storytelling

| Depending on who tells the story, the Imperial Valley in California is a trail of dreams, a cycle of harvests, the hand of God, a heart of fire. When I'm the one telling it, the tale begins with a train at the bottom of the sea.

Fishing for corvina on the Salton Sea with my dad in the early 1960s, I would stare long and hard into the water. "Tell me the story about the train," I'd say, and he would begin. "In the days before the sea, this whole area was a big salt flat, and they used to haul the salt out on trains." The boat would rock a little to port or starboard and the sea's surface would crease for a moment into the shape of an old steam locomotive. "When the waters came," he said, "they had to leave the train behind. It's still down there." I strained my eyes against the glare, looking for the lost salt train (see figure 1).

This book is about a California desert valley where a train sits mysteriously at the bottom of a sea. It is about how storytelling makes a place tangible in the human imagination—to those who live there, and to those who only hear the stories.

FIGURE 1. Leo Hetzel, *Imperial Valley Flood, 1926*.
Imperial County Historical Society.

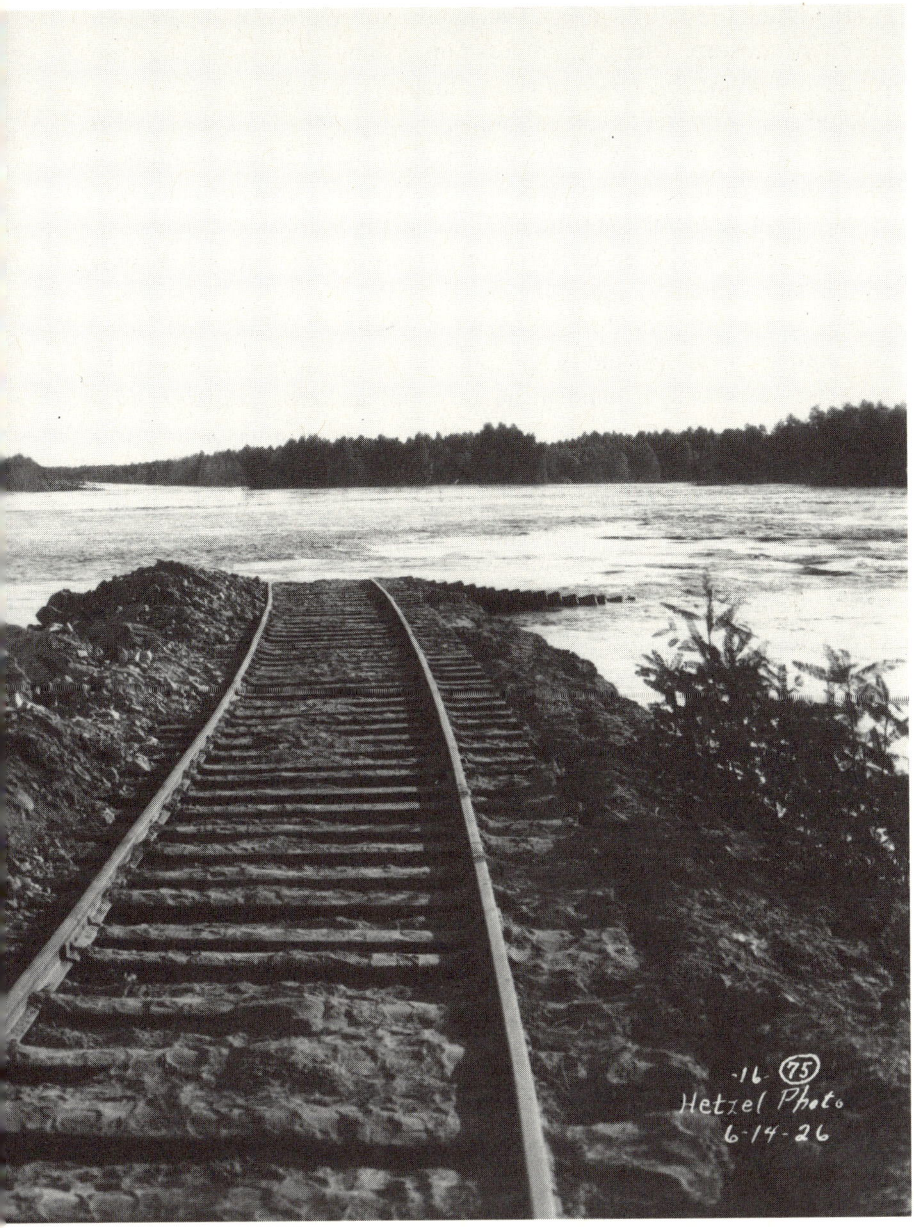
-16- 75
Hetzel Photo
6-14-26

This is how it is with all places, I've since discovered. A place exists as an inflection, a gesture. Often, it's conjured up at some distance, through the special present-making power of storytelling.

Storytelling in America has always grown out of the land. It is hard to imagine Henry Thoreau without Walden, John Ford without Monument Valley, Black Elk without the Black Hills. Storytelling brings a place into being. Without stories, a landscape is just so much rocks and sand and gravel, so many board feet. The same is true for us. Without stories, we ourselves are incomplete, *on* the land, not *of* it.

But land and story don't always come together easily. Many landscapes resist simple narratives, and the people who live in such places strain to connect themselves with their natural surroundings. *The Impossible Land* is about one such place and people. It gathers stories told in and about an arid region situated on the Mexican border in the southeast corner of California, christened the "Imperial Valley" by developers a hundred years ago. In the Imperial Valley, human beings and harsh environments have intertwined, giving birth to a century of strange chronicles—impossibly mythic, progressive, despairing.

As one of America's driest and most barren places, the valley originally offered little hope to its human inhabitants. It spawned only cautionary accounts of wandering, thirst, and loneliness. But when part of the valley became an irrigated "Eden" in the 1920s, off-putting desert stories were made over into parables of progress, opportunity, and money. Through good press, hard work, and sharp investment, the irrigated portion of the valley became one of the richest agricultural regions in California. In this well-watered oasis, storytellers touted the Imperial Valley as "the most important stage in the construction of an empire in the Southwest" (Howe and Hall 5). Their tales galvanized the nation, motivating one of America's largest water projects, which diverted the last remaining acre-feet of the Colorado River into this below-sea-level desert basin just before it entered Mexico and the Gulf of California.

The valley's sudden prosperity inspired a *New York Times* best seller and a Gary Cooper movie. Famous people went there to see an "inland empire" and partake of its splendor, its cheap land and dry air, its borderland mysteries—cantinas, bordellos, lawlessness. William Faulkner went drinking and duck hunting there, Humphrey Bogart made *Sahara* there, and Nathanael West died there.

Tales of affluence spurred an influx of immigrants from around the world—cheap labor willing to toil in the desert sun. In the 1920s, it was the

Japanese who made a go of it as tenant farmers, only to be rounded up in 1942, dispossessed of their farms, and sent to hastily constructed internment camps. Mexicans came, too, thousands making the dangerous desert crossing, picking up the harvest circuit as it dipped to the southernmost part of California for cantaloupes in June and lettuce in January.

By the 1950s, the valley was becoming a modern place. It was rural and agricultural, but its mechanized crop preparation, sophisticated irrigation system, and growing dependence on chemical fertilizers put it at the cutting edge of a new industry called "agribusiness." Its people were becoming modern too—at least in the demographic sense. Over the years, the valley had attracted a curious mix of Swiss dairymen, Filipino laborers, Okie refugees, and Chinese shopkeepers. While later Americans would brag or worry about their country's growing "multiculturalism," the Imperial Valley in the late 1950s was already a place where Hindi, Spanish, Mandarin, and Tagalog could be heard every day.

But the Imperial Valley also suffered the attendant hardships of modernity. For all of its pioneer visions of plenty, many of its inhabitants lived desperate lives. In education, employment, and opportunity, it routinely ranked last among California's fifty-eight counties. Its residents, when compared with the rest of California, are—according to a recent government report—"extraordinarily poor." Nearly 30 percent of its families with children are destitute, and one third of the kids who grow up there will never live above the poverty line. In 1990, almost half of its twenty-five-year-olds had not finished high school. With 40 percent of its working families spending at least two weeks a year in farm labor outside the valley, many children miss the first and last months of school. Education and child welfare workers in Imperial County report that almost 20 percent of the Latino children there are "linguistically isolated" from the English-speaking world of government and commerce. The monthly unemployment rate is the highest in the state, fluctuating between 24 percent and 31 percent. All of this in spite of the fact that Imperial County ranks among the top-ten agricultural producers in California, pulling in $900 million per year in agriculture revenues.

The interpenetration of these facts with the stories the valley's people tell about this place is what interests me. The hard facts of the Imperial Valley have been harnessed and negotiated by storytelling in much the same way that the arid desert has been partly reclaimed and managed by irrigation. In the following pages, I attempt to let the reader listen in on these ongoing conversations between human beings and this landscape, to liberate this land of hope and despair, humor and sadness, from its long entanglement in the vague, romantic myths of the place known broadly as the American West. By bringing the valley's conflicted conversations to the surface, *The Impossible Land* rediscovers a place whose real history—a complex weave of illegal immigration, ecological disaster, scientific innovation, and natural beauty—mirrors America's own as it enters the twenty-first century. In the process, it also rediscovers what it has taken for people to navigate the West's great transition into modern and even postmodern life.

Most students of the American landscape have relied on a concept called "regionalism" to describe the way Americans produce and consume stories about places like the Imperial Valley. As a field of scholarly study, regionalism explores the widely held belief that a certain geography and landscape gives the people who live there a shared experience and a shared set of values. As Wallace Stevens, the modernist American poet, put it,

> There are men whose words
> Are as natural sounds
> Of their places
> As the cackle of Toucans
> In the place of Toucans
> ("Anecdote of Men by the Thousands")

Celebrating the natural sounds of places has a long history in America. To speak of being *of* a place has its American roots in the environmentalist philosophy of intellectuals like Thomas Jefferson, who believed that the soil and climate, the verdure and vistas of this land would produce a brand new breed of humankind—Americans. Jefferson's spirit of place (the genius loci) was mysticism posing as science. It embraced the Indians, but disdained the Africans brought forcibly to America because they were not born of this "native" soil.

In the nineteenth century, literary regionalism emerged from mythological natural history to become a mode of storytelling in which capturing "local color" was the author's main concern. Yankees talked and acted like Yankees, lean and close, and Southerners talked and acted like Southerners, languid and drawling. Mark Twain's famous disclaimer on the opening page of *The Adventures of Huckleberry Finn* is partly a spoof on the vogue of such "dialect" fiction: "In this book a number of dialects are used . . . I make this explanation for the reason that without it many readers would suppose that all these characters were trying to talk alike and not succeeding."

Since Twain's day, regionalist literature has ebbed and flowed in popularity. In the 1930s, it was a growth industry. By the 1950s and 1960s, its heyday had passed, as a mobile postwar generation focused on the future, building new lives for themselves in small enclaves called suburbs, often far removed from their parents' rural homes. Now, at the beginning of the twenty-first century, regionalism is again exciting scholarly interest, this time for the way it blends place with identity politics. There is new interest in exploring the "connection between regionalism and ethnicity as forces in American literary history" (Karem 1).

There are many good reasons for thinking about story and place in the terms set down by literary regionalism—reasons related to why I, in Iowa, feel drawn to write a book about the California borderlands where I grew up. First, regional identification persists in contemporary America as a much-needed form of nostalgia. It shelters us modern and mobile Americans from the alienating forces of contemporary society, from postmodern hypertextualities and cyberspaces. As western historian Patricia Limerick observes, "In times of harried and disorienting change . . . regions [stabilize] the pulse, [slow] down the heartbeat, and ma[k]e life seem manageable again" (83).

A second reason region continues to fascinate us is that it continues to provide Americans with a special language of political opposition. In this country, where politicians love to talk about the homogenous voice of "the American people," speaking from one's region allows one to speak for oneself. In fact, it was the transplanted California regionalist Ronald Reagan who perfected the school of political rhetoric that defines itself by place, "outside the beltway," and by language, "plain talk." In America, where myths of national identity are rooted in a Protestant and "Pilgrim" past, speaking with the beat of a Spanish Catholic borderland or a French Creole bayou lets you in on the punch line from that old joke about Tonto and the Lone Ranger: "Whaddya mean *we*, white man?"

Finally, regionalism lures us urban, cosmopolitan grandsons and daughters of those who really did live down on the farm into an imaginary space where we find the ideals and history we think we lack. A large portion of regionalist literature, in fact, is written neither by nor for the people of a particular place, but rather by outsiders who wish to sell books in New York, Los Angeles, or Boston. Regionalism appeals to the urban and urbane reader because its celebration of dialect and place is also an elegy for the traditional cultures and "untouched" places that are fast disappearing in the face of modernization and urban sprawl. You can't fill the cities or scrape out a niche for suburbs if you don't transform place into *space*. You have to rezone the national imagination and relocate the mystical frontier to the pages of a book, which can then lament the whole *inevitable* process.

Richard Brodhead, a respected historian of American literature, describes the social and cultural dynamics that led to this regionalist formula. In an essay entitled "The Reading of Regions," he explains that "regionalism became a dominant genre in America ... at the moment when local-cultural economies felt strong pressure from new social forces, from a growingly powerful social model that overrode previously autonomous systems and incorporated them into translocal agglomerations" (119). These translocal agglomerations—things like corporations and, for Westerners, an increasingly monolithic federal government—created a "translocally incorporated social elite in place of older, local based gentry" (123). In response to these rapid changes, nineteenth-century regionalists produced a kind of "cultural elegy" for what had been lost.

One school of critical thought argues that the works of regionalists appealed to the emerging elite by providing them with a version of the exotic that was not as threatening as the new people and things they really feared—Italians, Jews, and Chinese; Buddhism, Judaism, and Catholicism. Their new appreciation of the deformed speech of hillbillies and all manner of semiliterates grew in part out of their desire to reaffirm their own "nonethnic status" (Brodhead 137). Regionalism allowed them to negate those who challenged their worldview by creating manageable sounds and images of what they themselves were not. By extension, readers could vicariously assume mastery over those imagined others the texts produced, thus confirming what the new cultural elite believed about themselves—that *they* were the center of cultural authority, and where they lived (New York, Boston, Washington, D.C.) was the locus of taste.

But while the cosmopolitan elites encouraged regionalism, they also relegated it to a fairly low rung on the ladder of literary achievement. Regionalist literature was considered too popular, too colloquial, and too mundane to rate the highest praises of the most educated critics and polished readers. Thus, as new regions gained a voice in the American literary canon, as Nebraska was heard through the words of Willa Cather, and the Midwest through those of Hamlin Garland, they were also cut off from the upper reaches of high art. The thoughts of the hinterlands might be quaint and odd, but they reflected an irredeemably backward way of life. Regionalism became a form of ethnography, field notes on retreating cultures cast in the cadences of fiction.

Of all the regions to serve these cosmopolitan desires, perhaps none has had more staying power or cultural mystique than the Southwest. My own southwesternmost corner of the Southwest is therefore uniquely suited to a close reading of how storytelling constructs a place, precisely because it is so unremarkable. Like some inland literary Galapagos, the Imperial Valley has incubated a microecology of the evolution of Southwest regionalism. Voices and stories have holed up there a long time, and beneath the valley's dusty, prosaic exterior, all the strife and violence and human aspirations that went into its settlement are now sedimented in the words and gestures of its storytellers.

Yet the Imperial Valley has never figured prominently in conventional southwestern regionalism. It is ignored in large part because it does not match the dominant regionalist fantasies about California and the Southwest. It is not a strip of coastal beach, a film noir city of night, or a Hollywood back lot. There are no missions there, and its desert, though arid and vast—a land of contrasts that are as sharp and distances that are as striking as any in the West—somehow lacks the glamour of Ship Rock and Chaco, Taos and Santa Fe.

Ironically, these disappointments are themselves the direct result of storytelling about what a desert ought to look like, and flow out of two strands of wish fulfillment that nineteenth-century Anglo Americans projected onto the West.

One involved the region's aridity, inspiring storytellers to weave fantastic visions of desert reclamation. The other entailed getting a handle on the desert's inhabitants—Hispanic and Native, Catholic and "pagan"—who seemed somehow out of the mainstream of American life.

Dealing with the barrenness of this land was a daunting task. The American deserts entered the immigrant European imagination by way of the Old Testament. Like the wilderness traversed by the Israelites in search of the Promised land, America's arid West was often depicted as a place of wandering and longing. A land of *confusión*, the Spaniards called it, and the people who lived there, a *gente sin razón* (a "people without intellect"). Anglo Americans, on the other hand, often viewed the desert as a continuation of the Plymouth Pilgrims' "horrid wilderness," of testing and trial, a place forsaken of God. Mormons gave their Utah outposts typological names like Moab and Ephraim. Even Horace Greeley's vaunted optimism met its match when faced with the American desert. Looking out over the Humboldt Valley of Nevada in 1859, Greeley could only wonder, "Who would stay in such a region one moment longer than he must?" (quoted in Teague 31).

Yet Patricia Limerick estimates that during the second half of the nineteenth century perhaps three hundred thousand Americans crossed the deserts of the Great Basin and the Far West (17). And even as they hated it, they saw in it immense possibilities. David Teague traces the stages by which Americans absorbed the deserts into their larger myths of national progress and racial destiny:

> First, deserts challenged the country to fulfill its obligation to spread Anglo-Saxon industrial civilization. The nation wouldn't have its continental house in order until the deserts were "reclaimed." Second, the deserts, because they were some of the harshest landscapes on the continent, became the ultimate place in which to pursue the "strenuous life" to work against the perceived moral and racial decay that Americans such as Roosevelt had begun to feel followed directly on the heels of civilization. Third, the desert, strange and different looking as it was, did not lend itself to immediate aesthetic appreciation. It became a challenge not only to the strength, practicality, and grit of the white Americans who came to it; it also challenged their higher sensibilities. (99)

For all the desert's seeming stasis and sterility, it inspired Europeans to feverish activity. The discovery of mineral wealth in the Far West in 1859 actually spurred travelers to choose the badlands as their final destination. The drought years of the 1880s inspired the great irrigation and reclamation movements of the 1890s, which aimed to bring distant mountain waters flooding into the barren wastes, uniting Old Testament vision with bourgeois progress. The progressive stories told about the arid West involved plots in which the desert "blossomed like a rose," and irrigation water "banished" the desert's silence "with the laughter of children" (Limerick 88).

Oddly, Anglo-Europeans also saw the desert in terms of race, telling stories that pitted heroic Anglo-Saxons against unwashed, uncivilized locals. Nineteenth-century explorers scorned the desert's Native peoples for accepting without a fight the marginal existence forced on them by the landscape. John C. Fremont thought that the single-minded struggle for survival brought on by desert living reduced such people to "mere animal creation." At the dawn of the new century, Ray Stannard Baker had an even more peculiar take on the situation. In 1902, echoing and refining a half-century of racist thinking about the region, he argued that "the Southwest is peopled by the very best Americans" because the deserts had not attracted immigration by "Italians, Russians or the lower class of Irish, most of whom are city dwellers" (Teague 103). There were Mexican and Indian laborers, to be sure, and even some Jewish traders, but in the desert, Anglo-Saxon purity was blissfully "segregated by the eternal law of evolutionary selection, with almost no substratum of the low-caste European foreigner to lower the level of civilization" (Teague 103).

To these interpreters of the desert West, the landscape cried out for racial and technological "reclamation." They produced thousands of pages of "propaganda" (in the words of noted irrigationist, William Ellsworth Smythe). Books like Smythe's *The Conquest of Arid America* (1895), and Harold Bell Wright's *The Winning of Barbara Worth* (1911) trumpeted the virtues of men dedicated, as Wright's narrator puts it, "to sav[ing] that land ... from itself." The heroes of these narratives, which ranged from "true" government reports to fictional stories, were always white men who faced the desert challenges of waste and want with manly fortitude.

Other storytellers, however, turned these racial notions on their head and romanticized the region's ethnic divergence from the American mainstream. Their desert fantasies played up its Catholic and Spanish past. In their tales, western dunes and mesas harkened back to an imaginary, idyllic time before Anglo American expansion, when the Spanish Missions anchored, as Helen Hunt Jackson put it in *Ramona* (1884), "the half barbaric, half elegant, wholly generous life led there by the Mexicans" (11).

Men like Charles Fletcher Lummis, city editor of the *Los Angeles Times* at the turn of the century, encouraged this softer "mission" vision of the West, organizing public celebrations—*fiestas*, he called them—which traded on romantic images of Spanish California life to provide a backdrop for civic boosterism as well as a cover for the Anglo American usurpation of the Californios' freedoms. Lummis founded a literary salon to go along with his mission pageants. The Arroyo Set, as it was called, strove to produce a regionalist literature that demonstrated Lummis's favorite thesis: "The power of sunshine to reinvigorate the racial energies of the Anglo Saxons" (Davis 27).

Even Mexican American elites had a stake in constructing this imaginary past of sleepy haciendas and dark-eyed Spanish maidens. Between the Spanish American War of 1898 and World War II, a powerful "Hispanidad" movement flourished in the cultural centers of the former Nueva Espana and Nueva Mexico. Like their Anglo American counterparts, the Latino elites of the Southwest needed some cultural way of distancing themselves from the Spanish empire that was being vilified in the U.S. press, as well as from the increasing numbers of immigrant laborers from Latin America. Derived from the literature produced by Spanish explorers during the golden ages of discovery and conquest, the regionalist literature they embraced offered dispossessed *Hispanos* a chance to instill national pride in the global community of Hispanics now divided by a history of diaspora and the crumbling of empire. Like their Anglo American counterparts, Latino cultural leaders wished to been seen as more purely European. They began to call themselves "Spanish" instead of Mestizo or Mexican. In the first decades of the twentieth century, they too enacted elaborate celebrations of the Spanish Imperial past with a series of public festivals called "Old Spanish Days." They too strove to create a regionalist canon, founding in New Mexico in 1929 the Quivira Society, a literary publishing venture dedicated to reprinting old Spanish imperial texts such as the *Viajes Marítimos*, the *Crónicas*, the *Meorias*, and the *Visitas* (Gutiérrez 244–45).

To the literary avant-garde of the early twentieth century, the desert West conversely offered the perfect locale for divesting American art and storytelling once and for all of its false romance. In the 1880s, as the transcontinental railroad linked east to west through the great deserts of Arizona and California, elite writers and readers of magazines like *The Century* and *Harper's* could enjoy breezy tours of the region "from a car window." By the turn of the century, an important aesthetic shift had begun. Intellectuals began turning west to the deserts for "truth." The western deserts proffered a new sort of "reality" based on quiet, solitude, and authenticity. Patricia Limerick observed, "To the degree that one found civilization unattractive, one could admit the most intractable of environments for its purity. The convention of the desert as 'the most real' of landscapes carried through" (168). In *The of Land of Little Rain* (1903), for example, Mary Austin attacked the "unrealistic" regionalist writings of nineteenth-century writers like Brete Harte, assuring her readers that they would not be subjected to Harte's "pastoral gloss," but rather would experience the West in all its "elemental violence" (40).

Within a few years of the dawning of the twentieth century, all of these dreams—of elemental truth, of pastoral romance, of desert reclamation—would merge into the one word that still unites them today: Southwest. It is a word that threatens to permanently fix a diverse and difficult geography within the limited cosmopolitan and ethnographic gaze of the outsider. As Reed Way Dasenbrock has pointed out, the question is not so much what is the Southwest, but rather: "Southwest of What?" The answer has most often been, "southwest of time," or, "southwest of all our problems."

To late-twentieth-century American mystics, the New Age seekers who worship crystals and what they believe is "Native American Spirituality," the lines of the earth's sacred power *must* flow through Sedona, and the art that spiritualizes their middle-class lives *must* come from Taos or Santa Fe. Their imaginary Southwest, the Southwest of cuisine and furniture, is curiously without history, despite its appeals to the past of Chaco and Mesa Verde. There is no Pueblo Revolt, no Mexican War, no gangs, no methamphetamines, no sinking water table, no agricultural runoff in this Southwest.

The reality is that in Albuquerque and Nogales, Las Cruces and Yuma, it is the region's colonial history—a history of forced migration, dispossession, poverty, entrepreneurial laissez faire politics, and racist propaganda—that has determined the flow of power, the sinking of spirits, the colors of everyday life. Viewed from this perspective, Southwest might just as well mean "left out." Scarred by an eighteen-hundred-mile international border, the region is, in Gloria Anzaldúa's words, *"una herida abierta* [an open wound] where the Third World grates against the first and bleeds" (3). California's Imperial Valley lies at the center of this other Southwest, the one from which America averts its eyes, the one it pretends does not exist. It crystallizes the forces of colonial history like no other place in the Golden State, and its shocking divergence from the California dream serves to throw these forces into high relief.

In order to recover the Imperial Valley's forgotten stories—and thereby recover the "other" Southwest—we must begin to think in new ways about storytelling and the meaning of places such as the Imperial Valley in the national imagination. We must supplement the received perspectives and terminology of literary regionalism with the concepts and approaches of the New Western History and emerging studies in the anthropology of place. Both fields are particularly well suited to discussing places like the Imperial Valley, because both take it as a given that the history of any place must be told from the point of view of the colonized and oppressed as well as that of its official storytellers. Scholars in these fields understand that popular culture and nontraditional forms of expression are as important as those charted in cosmopolitan best sellers.

Such new approaches offer, first, new definitions of place itself. Richard White, one of the founders of the New Western History, has defined places such as the Imperial Valley as "spatial realit[ies] constructed by people" (White and Findlay x). Such places are first and foremost "human creations," and the most common mode of human creation is the story. With their ability to project a "mental imposition of order, a parcelization of the earth's surface," stories have the power to transform "space—an abstraction—into something more specific and limited" (White and Findlay x).

Reorienting our perspective also involves recognizing that places like the Imperial Valley are profoundly modern and subject to change, no matter how "elemental" their geology or "timeless" life may appear there. They are marked by the same "acute . . . conditions of exile, displacement, diasporas, and inflamed borders" that have inspired anthropologists elsewhere to focus on the centrality of deterritorialization, migration, and mobility to place studies (Basso and Feld 4). In modern places across the globe—from the Imperial Valley to the Darfur region of Sudan—human beings are increasingly being forced to orient themselves to landscapes in nontraditional ways, sometimes dwelling for long periods in one location, at other times migrating into and out of the homelands of others. New and contested national boundaries have been drawn haphazardly across traditional migratory routes. Border fences sequester formerly gathered foodstuffs; border guards determine personal identity in unacceptable ways.

These modern circumstances of place produce corresponding tensions between the quotidian details of human lives lived in a particular geography and the forces exerted on them from outside. Contemporary anthropologists see the interrelationship of people and land as "cultural process[es] that [are] dynamic, multisensual, and constantly oscillating between a foreground of everyday empowerment and a background of social potential" (Appadurai 6). This gap between the foreground and background of lives lived in any landscape is itself an index of a more general crisis of modernity that one anthropologist has characterized as the "betweeness of place" (Entrikin 1).

In addition to providing a new sense of the complexities involved in how human beings experience place, New Western History and the anthropology of place offer us the chance to unravel the "vocabularies of looking" that went into making the Imperial Valley "visible" to different groups of people. As painters and photographers began to document both the valley's desert vistas and its engineering accomplishments, as advertisers began circulating flyers stuffed with words such as *magic, remarkable*, and *Imperial*, developers, growers, laborers, and tourists all became fluent in saying what it was they sought here and seeing what they said they saw. In the Imperial Valley, the sheer number of these vocabularies offers a fascinating index of how people have struggled over the region's resources, how they have fought "wars of position" to win the right to tell the story of this irrigated desert basin that best suits their senses of self, and their economic and cultural needs.

In the following literary history of the Imperial Valley, I will attempt a synthesis of these various vocabularies and the stories they have engendered, tacking between insider and outsider perspectives. In the process, I hope to articulate a different set of relationships between self and place, genius and locus, than that which has informed most regionalist literary study in the past. Imperial Valley stories are not so much *products* of a region or *projections* of cosmopolitanism as *relations* of individual human imaginations to the material conditions of a landscape in a specific historical milieu. This perspective demands a view of region in which place is never fixed and the stories about it never quite finished, never certain. As the Kiowa storyteller Scott Momaday observes, stories "are not subject to the imposition of such questions as true or false, fact or fiction. Stories are realities lived and believed" (3). It is partly because stories are based in faith that I have chosen to focus on them here. Attaching oneself to a particular landscape requires a leap of faith, but it is nonetheless also a leap into history and the material reality of survival. The degree to which diverse peoples have taken such leaps, lived their stories and believed them, is the degree to which the Imperial Valley has come into historical being.

In the chapters that follow, I will focus on some of the stories that have sprung up from a very limited geographic space, the Imperial Valley, during a very distinct period of time, the twentieth century. After briefly outlining the historical and ecological facts of the Lower Colorado Desert basin, I move to a consideration of three popular strands of cosmopolitan storytelling about the valley. The first, from 1901, is credited with establishing a "desert aesthetic" movement in America. This set of stories about the Imperial Valley may be said to have made desert vistas palatable and even sought after in this country. The second, which begins about a decade later, mythologizes desert reclamation as a moral imperative for America. It is the storytelling tradition that lies behind the masthead of the Imperial Valley's first newspaper: "Water is King, Here is its Kingdom." The third emerged in the 1930s and might be called the story of "human erosion." This strand was spun from the mouths of dust-bowl refugees and woven together with images taken of them by Farm Security Administration photographers documenting the Great Depression.

The rest of the book explores the storytelling traditions of the "others" who appear in the background of these popular storylines. In this section, I look at the stories of Japanese Americans who farmed the valley in the 1930s and were eventually imprisoned in desert internment camps in the 1940s. Another set of stories follows Chicano/a and Mexican storytelling in and around the valley. I end with Native American migration stories that recount the mythic emergence and experiences of the "First people" of this desert land. Their stories bring us full circle, giving voice to both the most modern and most ancient human utterances of this impossible land.

I called this book *The Impossible Land* because the Imperial Valley, like most places, resists easy definition. That was true over two hundred years ago when the first Europeans set eyes on it. The Spanish explorer Juan Baptista De Anza and his men found the valley's harsh landforms and deceptive optics disorienting. As they struggled toward Mount Signal, a rugged 2,500-foot peak that sits astride today's international border, it appeared to move away from them. After two days of marching, in which they seemingly drew no closer to their destination, they named it Cerro del Imposible (Impossible Hill) and turned back.

This disorienting quality remains true today, even though there are undeniably real and material presences here, rocks and sand and irrigated farmlands. The wide All-American canal, glittering improbably across the valley's eastern sand dunes is a kind of self-evident truth. So too are the bundles of carrots and asparagus, the wintertime head lettuce, that appear like clockwork on my Iowa grocer's shelves, bearing the real names of the packers and growers who live and work in the valley today. But it is important to remember as well the visions and myths about the place because they are sometimes just as real as its produce and progress. A mythic vision of the valley, spun out in advertising and booster novels at the turn of the twentieth century, fed into a real disaster that flooded the valley and changed its ecosystem forever. In a similar way, the stories we tell ourselves about immigrants that hazard that desert, crossing the invisible line in the sand that separates the United States from Mexico to work in the Imperial Valley, have far-reaching, physical effects on this place. Now, in the first decade of the twenty-first century, the stories we recite about them are dire, and the results substantial. Soon there will be a fifteen-foot concrete barrier along the valley's southern border, lipped on the Mexican side with a three-foot overhang to make it harder to climb. More than one resident on the Mexican side of the border has remarked with some sadness that "it will be like the Berlin Wall."

In the following chapters I open up my own conversations with this "impossible land," engaging stories I've overheard and read about this place. They are historical and linguistic, real and imaginary. Not all of them are true, but there is some truth in all of them. Like a geologist's exploratory trench, this book cuts into the layered strata of one hundred years of storytelling in this irrigated desert valley. And like a wise geologist, I know that even if a certain stratum has been buried a hundred years, its life deep below the surface continues to affect the topography and landforms above. At any moment—tomorrow or in another hundred years—an earthquake or a flood might thrust it again into the light, arching its metamorphic back once more into view. That inland sea might then drain away into the fissured earth, baring the calcified remains of an old salt train, shimmering uncertainly in the desert sun.

1 The Impossible Land

| Let's start with some facts. Carved out from the much larger Colorado River Desert by politics and geography, the Imperial Valley is a six thousand-square-mile palm-shaped basin in Southeast California that stretches from the Mexican border to U.S. Interstate 10 (see figure 2). Containing some of the most arid land in the United States, it is one of the country's most sparsely populated regions. Bounded to the east by the Colorado River, broad and silty from the 1,450-mile trek from its headwaters in the Rocky Mountain National Forest, it is walled in to the west by the Santa Rosa and San Jacinto mountains of the California peninsular range. To the south lies Mexico, whose ninety-mile border is etched out by an imaginary line meandering across an indistinguishable desert landscape.

In the withering midday light, this land is especially featureless. Even the slight depressions made by gravel washes and bumps of low mesquite cast no shadow and give no texture. But come dusk, that which appeared flat and white grows wrinkled and furrowed, as shadows spread across the dunes to give this lifeless place an aura of deliberate accomplishment. Where the desert meets the first cultivated swatches of alfalfa and Sudan grass, the shadows themselves are transformed—first by the sharp-edged

FIGURE 2. Satellite photograph of the Imperial Valley. Data available from U.S. Geological Survey/EROS, Sioux Falls, SD.

silhouettes of dune crest and ironwood branch, then by the softer adumbration of salt cedar and windrow.

The subtlety of the variations result from the fact that the Imperial Valley is an ecological transition zone. It sits between the Mojavian desert system to the north—with its closed basin and limited drainage—and the Sonoran system to the south, where extensive drainage creates, among other things, huge "forests" of giant Saguaro cactus made famous as symbols of the desert Southwest in Hollywood movies. Of all the Colorado Desert valleys, the Imperial is the lowest of the low. At some points it sinks to more than two hundred feet below sea level, the remnant of a deep Pleistocene furrow called the Salton Trough. The trough has, over the centuries, created a special microclimate, its abnormal depth acting as a kind of atmospheric vacuum, drawing in summer rain and harboring mild winters. Its ecological effect, largely indiscernible to the passing traveler, is significant enough for botanists to consider this area a unique biological subregion—the Lower Colorado—its boundaries marked by the appearance of Ocotillo and Woodland Wash plant communities.

To the jaundiced eye of the freeway motorist trying to get from Phoenix to San Diego on Interstate 8, the Lower Colorado appears a monotonous monochrome, perennially dusty, even bleak. Crossing the desert by freeway, a driver flies over washes on two-lane overpasses that elide a millennia of geologic stories chronicled in the gravel deposited below. In the upper reaches of a wash, one might find two-million-year-old gravel bars; in the lower reaches, rocks deposited fifteen thousand years ago. Some stones have rested untouched since Anza's expedition. Others were unearthed just yesterday.

Heading north toward Palm Springs, the same driver could catch a glimpse on the western foothills of another geologic wonder. Dark water stains mark the fifty-thousand-year-old shoreline of Lake Cahuilla, an inland waterway that once inundated the Salton Trough and the two-thousand-square-mile area around it. At a rise in the desert floor called Superstition Mountain, along the western fringe of the valley, fossilized clam beds and eerie, eroded sea stacks testify to an antediluvian past.

Over the centuries, as Lake Cahuilla receded, the great Colorado River that carved out the valley's eastern border periodically overflowed its banks and found its own level in the Salton Basin and its surrounding arroyos. By 1680, when the Pueblo people of New Mexico rose against the Spaniards and cast them out, Lake Cahuilla had withered into a salt flat, but the river invaded the newly formed desert at irregular intervals. In 1905, the ancient lake returned as a sea. That spring, the Colorado River shifted its course, breaking through wooden diversions engineers had erected on its banks, sending silty, chocolate-brown floodwaters down long-forgotten drainages toward the lowest portion of the valley, the Salton Trough. The Southern Pacific Railroad Company, whose trains ran into the saline flats to pick up loads of salt, moved swiftly to dam up the diversion, but they were too late. Old Lake Cahuilla was reborn as the Salton Sea, becoming the largest inland body of salt water in the United States.

Beneath the ancient lakebed, there are deeper, more dangerous mutations taking place. Rippling through the valley's core is the San Andreas Fault, a ragged seam that threatens to sink coastal California and bring the waters of the Gulf of California racing back into the valley to reclaim Lake Cahuilla's shores. In 1940, a quake measuring 7 on the Richter scale rocked the valley, killing five people and causing a half a million dollars in damage. Once, in the late 1970s, the valley shook day after day for over a week. Called an "earthquake swarm" by the scientists who came to study it, the weeklong rumbling gave valley residents a strange kind of sea legs. Cracks fingered out across walls and highways. Here and there a farmer would come across some country road bubbling up with magma-heated mud. By the weekend, news crews had become a common sight and trucks labeled "Cal Tech" could be seen parked at coffee shops in the early morning.

Like the valley's geology, its human population was active long before Columbus stumbled on his new world. Twenty thousand years ago, along the slowly receding shoreline of Lake Cahuilla, the first people lived what anthropologists term "a simple culture." Stone tools found in the Lower Colorado date from 48,000 to 6000 BPE, and in October 1971, a professor of archaeology from Imperial Valley College unearthed a burial mound that had sheltered human remains for twenty thousand years. Scientists determined the skeleton to be that of a male in his late teens, a little over five feet tall. They called him "Yuha Man," after the section of the desert where he had lain for millennia. A few years later, a perfectly preserved ancient footprint was discovered in the sun-baked sand along the old Lake Cahuilla beach.

When the waters of Lake Cahuilla receded, these people retreated to the desert's fringes. By the time of European exploration, few lived in the Yuha Desert permanently. It was hot, and there was too little to eat. The valley had become an obstacle—something to be crossed and overcome—to reach the cool forests of the Coastal Range or the fertile banks of the Colorado.

Three major cultural groups made crossing this desert a way of life. To the east, along the banks of the Colorado, the Quechan (Yuma) people clustered in mobile settlements, planting and harvesting maize, beans, and squash in the river bottoms during the months when the seasonal flood tides receded. To the northwest, ranging over a varied landscape of mountains and desert were the Cahuilla, whose twenty-four-hundred-square-mile traditional territory is located in the geographic center of Southern California. Scientists named the Imperial Valley's ancient lake after them. Between Quechan and Cahuilla, at the Imperial Valley's below-sea-level center, were the Tipai, who settled along the sloughs that feathered out into the desert from the Colorado's springtime floods. Like their Quechan neighbors to the east, they farmed rich, silt-laden arroyos after yearly floodwaters receded. Like the Cahuilla, the Tipai settlements along the Yuma trail from the Colorado to the Pacific placed them at a crossroads of intertribal travel and trade.

An historical marker out on old Highway 78 in the northeast part of the valley commemorates this era of native migration. There, in the low light of sunset, across a cropped mesa of burnt lava rock, you can just make out the faint depression of a trail that traverses the arid expanse to and from the Colorado. The footpath hugs a wash whose solid stone bottom has been bowled and cupped by centuries of periodic flooding.

Human migrations across the Lower Colorado went on for thousands of years. As the Mexican empire of Tula fell and Cortez laid siege to Tenochtitlán, the people of the desert kept moving. While the Spaniards invaded the New Mexico Pueblos, occupied them, and were cast out by Popé and his followers—the people of the Imperial Valley kept crossing. It wasn't until 1776 that the Spanish conquistador Juan Baptista de Anza, seeking an overland route from Arizona to the California coast, claimed this desert in the name of Spain.

To the earliest Europeans, the mobile life of the desert people, punctuated by flood and drought, seemed *unreasonable*. The land they inhabited appeared impossibly confusing. Father Font, a Franciscan who traveled with the Anza expedition in 1776, declared it "a deadly place."

Although Anza crossed the Imperial Valley several times, and he and his men filled over eight diaries with stories about the place, no European would stay on to settle there for another hundred years. As the American colonies grew into the United States and began pushing westward, the Spaniard's route remained little used by Europeans. The Yuma people who lived along the banks of the Colorado successfully repelled all invaders until 1826.

Americans, who took over this land of confusion after the Mexican War of 1848, didn't fare much better than their Spanish predecessors. General Kearney passed through the valley in 1846–47, opening the way for gold seekers needing a winter route into California. But only a few soldiers and scientists such as John Audubon, Herbert Blake, and Joseph Ives actually sought out the harsh desert and tried to understand it. Audubon, son of the famous naturalist, was no stranger to rugged travel and bizarre landscapes when he first set eyes on the Imperial Valley in 1849. What he saw there, however, paralyzed his reason. "There was not a tree to be seen, nor the least sign of vegetation," Audubon recorded, "and the sun pouring down on us made our journey seem twice the length it really was" (166). He called it "the most melancholy scene" he had witnessed since leaving the Rio Grande.

It was California gold that finally changed Anglos' opinions about the place, inspiring new expeditions across sand dunes and salt flats. By the 1850s, the entrepreneurial schemes of new explorers threatened the end of the traditional life ways of the Cahuilla, Quechans, and Tipai. The valley became a political region, organized by bureaucracies located hundreds of miles away. Fort Yuma, described as "the Botany Bay of military stations," was founded on its eastern edge in 1851. Immigrants from Sonora and the United States began to trickle over the old De Anza trails, increasing in numbers so much that by 1858, more than twenty thousand had made the desert crossing.

It wasn't long before regular routes were established between the settled areas of New Mexico and the towns of the California coast. Gold seekers and adventurers gave way to tourists and permanent settlers. The San Diego and San Antonio Mail Lines soon improvised a stage route through the valley. Locals called it the "Jackass Mail" because some sections were so rough that passengers had to disembark the coach and mount mules.

Little by little, passersby began to discover beauty there. In 1871, bestselling author John Ross Browne paused in a breathless narrative of his adventures in Apache country to gaze on the Imperial Valley. "I scarcely remember to have seen a wilder country," Browne told his readers. By his account, the valley was a showplace, with "barren hills of gravel and sandstone, flung up at random out of the earth, strange jagged mountain-peaks in the distance; yellow banks serrated by floods; sea-shells glittering in the wavy sand-fields that lie between" (47). It was chaos on a cosmic scale, yet Browne found "a peculiar charm . . . in the rich atmospheric tints that hung over this strange land, and the boundless wastes that lay outspread before us; and I drank in with an almost childish delight the delicate and exquisite odors that filled the air" (47).

Browne's romantic alchemy, transforming boundless waste into a delicate tapestry of colors and scents, marked the beginning of a pivotal change in attitude toward America's arid regions. In the late nineteenth century, people began to appreciate desert air and desert colors. Even more than Taos or Santa Fe or Death Valley, the Lower Colorado—suddenly accessible by train and stage and located in the middle of California's most important winter overland route—captured the imaginations of America's first desert aesthetes (see figure 3).

While artists and philosophers were awakening to the Imperial Valley's desolate beauty, others began to see it as an investment opportunity. The progressive era, epitomized by Teddy Roosevelt's promotion of "the strenuous life" and American plans to dig a ditch across Central America connecting the Caribbean Sea and Pacific Ocean, began in the first decades of the twentieth century. Projects for the improvement of man and nature abounded, and the Imperial Valley seemed ripe for "progress." George Chaffey, a Canadian engineer who made a name for himself in the 1880s by building an electric power plant to light Los Angeles, was put in charge of "reclaiming" the Lower Colorado. Chaffey's plan was to divert water from the Colorado River into the low-lying Imperial Valley, where, as a result of centuries of periodic flooding, the desert was rich in alluvial topsoil. With just a little water, the desert would—according to the Old Testament prophet and modern boosters—"blossom as a rose."

The engineering was tricky. Chaffey had to build special diversionary gates—something like miniature dams—that would shift the flow of the river water into canals on the valley floor. The topography was such that Chaffey had to direct his channel through Mexican territory. It ran parallel to the international border for fifty miles before turning north into the United States near the present-day towns of Calexico and Mexicali. During the twenty-two months Chaffey oversaw the project, four hundred miles of canals and laterals were built. On May 14, 1901, Colorado riffles began flowing into the valley, and the desert indeed began to bloom.

In the spring of 1903, twenty-five thousand acres in the Imperial Valley were in agricultural production. By fall, that number had grown fourfold. With a settler population of about two thousand now clamoring for water, it seemed that Chaffey had perhaps done his job too well. The demand far exceeded the supply his prototype system could provide.

There were other problems as well. Unbeknownst to the schemers and settlers, the waters of the Colorado had, in the few short years since the diversion was built, begun to pile up silt to a depth of four feet in front of Chaffey's diversion, slowing the flow of the water into the valley to a trickle. Chaffey's engineers compensated for this shortfall during the river's ebb season by dredging a small bypass around the gate to allow the now much-lower water

FIGURE 3. Leo Hetzel, *Imperial Valley Plank Road*. Imperial County Historical Society.

Hetzel Photo

to feed the newly reclaimed fields. But by 1904, even this bypass had silted up. Officials decided to open a new gate, called Intake #3, some four miles deeper into Mexican territory, taking advantage of an easier-to-dredge route. Certain that high water was not due along this stretch of the Colorado until at least April or May, they were confident they could close the new intake just as soon as the winter crops were in.

They were wrong. The first flood came unexpectedly in February 1905 and before work crews could close the bypass, new floods arrived to sweep away their sandbags and reed mats. Throughout the spring, floodwaters kept coming. By June, the workers abandoned their stations as day after day, nine-thousand-second feet of water rushed north from the Mexican cutoff into the Salton Basin.

The failure of Intake #3 forever changed the natural landscape of the Imperial Valley. It produced two north-running rivers—the Alamo and the New—that flowed out of Mexico into the desert, as well as the Salton Sea, the largest inland body of salt water in the United States. It also changed the political tenor of the valley. No longer convinced that free-market capitalism, developers, or the federal government could be trusted with their dream of an oasis, Imperial Valley citizens banded together in 1911 to form the Imperial Irrigation District, a trusteeship designed to oversee the construction and maintenance of the huge water project.

Those are the facts, but they don't even come close to telling the valley's whole story. Long before the engineers were finished, the storytellers were moving in, transforming Chaffey's careful calculations into progressive-era mythology.

Blackburn's Map of Imperial County, dated 1943, provides an index of the degree to which storytelling took hold over the enormous water project, transforming the Lower Colorado Desert into an *imperial* valley (see figure 4). The map presents a valley ripe for speculation, gridding Anza's "impossible land" into saleable 360-acre sections. What most strikes the contemporary viewer are its colorful array of place names, a tangible catalogue of one possible "vocabulary of looking" at the Salton Basin.

Designations like Chocolate and Chuckwalla, Picacho and Superstition mark the valley's peaks. Facing each other along the Mexican border are the American town of Calexico and Baja's capital city of Mexicali, fanciful sobriquets that graft bits of California and Mexico together in a kind of linguistic handshake. Further north, there is El Centro—"the center"—the county seat, where the interstate crosses the desert from San Diego to Yuma. A few miles up the road is Imperial; pioneer-day photographs of this

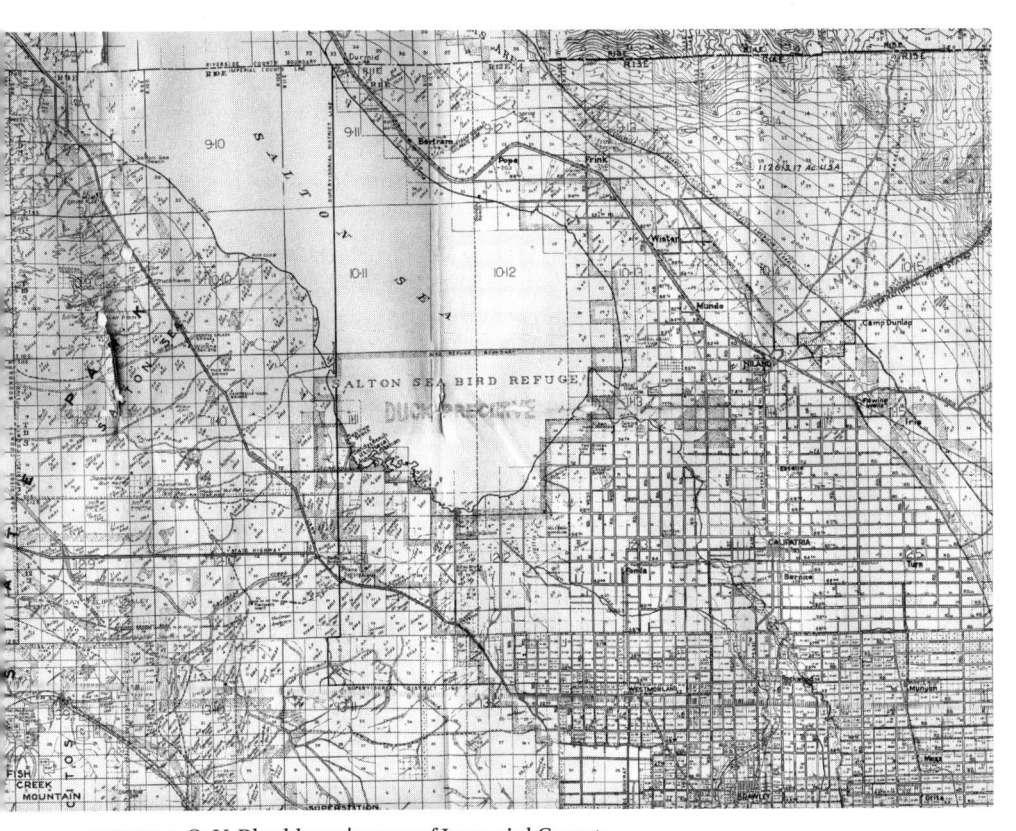

FIGURE 4. O. V. Blackburn's map of Imperial County.

town show a flat, treeless place whose name never quite conjured up the empire it was supposed to epitomize. At the valley's northern periphery lies Calipatria—*Pro Patria California*, this town says. Spread out along the valley's perimeter are other, abandoned hamlets whose names embody their founders' hopes and fears—Dixieland, Poppy, Sidewinder, Sunset Siding.

Early apologists for irrigation likened the shape of the irrigated valley to the palm of one's hand—the *Mano de Dios*, novelist Harold Bell Wright called it. Another writer described it like this:

> Face north and hold your left hand before you, palm uppermost, slightly cupped. If your fingers and thumbs are held together as you sit so you will have before you a very fair relief map of the Imperial Valley. The fingers will represent the Chuckawalla, or Chocolate range of mountains fringing the desert on the north and northeast, your thumb will represent the Coast range and the Santa Rosa mountains, with San Jacinto, San Bernardino, San Gorgonio (Old Greyback) about at the end of your thumb. Then the very palm of your hand is the Imperial Valley with the Salton Sea of the present day on the "mount" at the base of the first finger. If the lines of your hand are marked perhaps you can imagine that one known to palmists as the "life" line is the course of New River. (Howe and Hall 57)

It is a magical formula, a spell or a ritual intended to place the desert in the palm your hand, to give you power over it, allowing you to raise it as an offering to God.

Or so the story goes.

Seen from a different angle, another sort of kingdom emerges, an earthbound land that bears the scars of mindless entrepreneurialism, whose people are among the poorest and least educated in all of California. Sometimes, heading down the Mountain Springs grade into the south end of the valley, you get an overwhelming feeling of emptiness. It's a quick three-thousand-foot drop into a monochrome of sand and haze. At the foot of the grade, the air is oppressive, even in winter when it's cool and dry. One hundred feet below sea level, you feel the weight of the world pressing in.

Coming in from the north, the descent is more gradual, but no less unnerving. First come acres and acres of wind turbines bristling atop the hills at Cabazon. Next, billboards touting the Palm Springs golf courses, casinos, and time-shares. The road improves, the tax base showing through its fresh asphalt and yellow reflective lines, crisp off-ramps, and roadside landscaping. You're not really in the Imperial Valley yet. This is the transition zone between Los Angeles and everything else. When you hit Indio, though, you realize that you're entering another world. The town's name says it all.

The superhighway peters out. Detour signs direct you onto a circuit of county highways and country roads. Soon you are on what locals call old Highway 86, marked by deep alkaline borrow pits on either side, walled in by impenetrable citrus and date groves. Houses are makeshift affairs of corrugated tin, tires, and plywood, or old motor homes. The parts that are painted remind you of Mexico, with its palette of not-quite pastels. Summer or winter, there are no children playing in the yard. There is no yard. Only here and there, rusted-out farm implements and snarling Rotweilers.

The silence is palpable. At sixty-five miles an hour, windows rolled up tight, you can't hear dogs or children anyway. It's the kind of undersea silence you experience in speeding through any number of America's wastelands, and it is out of this silence that the Imperial Valley's stories were born. Yet the silence of other places doesn't have quite the same feeling one experiences here most of the time, descending into the valley at the beginning of the twenty-first century, the great water project accomplished, the ancient desert enduring at its fringes. Open yourself to that feeling, and the stories rush out hard and fast.

The first published story about the valley, John C. Van Dyke's *The Desert* (1901) is set just about here, where Highway 86 skirts the metallic shores of the Salton Sea. In those days it was still a great salt flat called the Salton Basin, and Van Dyke found its desolation inspiring. Down here, "the weird solitude, the great silence, the grim desolation," beckoned the storyteller, begging him to fill this arid void with words.

2 "Silence and Desolation"

| The Imperial Valley's first twentieth-century Euro American storyteller was not a storyteller at all, really. He was John C. Van Dyke, professor of art history at Rutgers University in New Jersey, who traveled in the same elite New York social circles as Edith Wharton.

His story wasn't much of a story either. It was more of a treatise about the state of American aesthetics and the American landscape at the turn of the new century. Van Dyke's published impressions of the Imperial Valley gave rise to a pristine palette of surprising earth tones never before explored by artists, American or otherwise. They schooled the reader in modernist optics—a dance of mirage and shadow, ochres and gunmetal, oxides of copper, iron, and manganese. They challenged the old Hudson River School verities of picturesque wooded landscapes, and Van Dyke believed, offered America redemption from a wasting sensibility that had softened its art and its thinking into sentimental mush.

Although Van Dyke claimed in a letter to his publisher to have just spent "two years in the sands with Mexicans and rattlesnakes for company," Peter Wild and Neil Carmony have established that he probably worked up most of his Imperial Valley story sitting at his brother's ranch in the Mojave Desert.

In comfort, he sat and mused about desert views taken in from dining car windows and hotel verandas. A classic cosmopolitan.

Still, the book he produced about the Lower Colorado, *The Desert* (1901), is praised by critics today for its pivotal role in bringing about a cultural shift in America. Van Dyke managed to channel American attitudes away "from traditional scorn to viewing the Southwest as a region to be appreciated for its wild beauty" (Wild and Carmony 1). Thus, although the Colorado River Desert would eventually be eclipsed by Arizona's Monument Valley and New Mexico's Taos as the must-have desert location, it inspired the first major aesthetic appreciation of an American desert landscape.

The impetus for this cultural shift came from historian Frederick Jackson Turner's now-famous 1893 announcement that the West was "closed." The wild frontier, he claimed, had been tamed by private property. Certainly the West wasn't closed, and everybody knew it, but Turner was being provocative to highlight a trend that he and other intellectuals thought they detected in American society. Turner felt America was going to hell in a handcart, losing its moral bearings, showing signs of "racial decay." The "frontier hypothesis," as it has since been named, was a theory about America founded on the notion that a society's constant forward progress depended on a vast unpeopled and undeveloped frontier. It was this open, creative space that had inspired Anglo-Saxon Americans to great things. Thus, an America off her progressive course could only mean one thing: there was no frontier left to inspire her.

People like Turner looked around and found a West that had reneged on the Founders' dreams of an agrarian republic. The West hadn't given rise to the nucleated settlements and yeoman farmers that Jefferson had envisioned. One half of the land in the Far West was undeveloped and owned by the federal government. Most of the West was too arid to farm on the eastern model, and deserts and mines and boomtowns—arenas of free play for new entrepreneurial forces Jefferson could never have imagined—resisted the old mythologies of Pilgrim people and virgin land.

Yet it was precisely this failure of the West to match the Jeffersonian ideal that made it so aesthetically attractive to many Americans at the dawn of the twentieth century. Not having bought into the myths of frontier and progress to begin with, these Americans welcomed the end of civilization as they knew it. They sought a fresh start, a primitive place in which to begin the social experiment over again. Casting about for ways to make their formerly "New World" new again, artists and writers struck on the West—especially its forbidding deserts—as the ideal empty canvas to be filled with words and images with the power to challenge their parents' Victorian values. In the cosmopolitan centers of America, both Anglo and Hispanic American cultural entrepreneurs began to shape a regionalist literature and art in which the desert served as the centerpiece. Their arid West was a *newer* new world, one whose elemental forces dramatized their renewed hope that "the land may breed . . . qualities in her human offspring, not tritely to 'try,' but to do" (Austin 3).

John C. Van Dyke's biography hints at why he gave himself over to the task of transforming the American deserts into something the general public could call "beautiful." He was one among many artists, scientists, and writers who flooded into the arid Southwest as a new breed of entrepreneurs and frontiersmen, who mixed the avocation of geologist or botanist with that of travel writer and philosopher. They were a mixed bag of artists, sightseers, and con men, and Van Dyke's own complex motives for going to the desert reflect the collage of reasons that prompted the late-century cultural movement west. In ill health, and having fathered an illegitimate child in New York's polite society, Van Dyke hastily booked passage on a train to his brother's Mojave Desert ranch. Before he left, he met with Andrew Carnegie, from whom he received hush money to pass on to labor organizer James McLuckie somewhere out in the anonymous mesa country, far from the prying eyes of muckraking journalists.

Van Dyke had a lifelong tendency to hit the road when things got dicey or dull. A confirmed bachelor, he shared the restless mobility of a whole class of post-Victorian Americans, a generation, in Edith Wharton's view, of "wan beings as richly upholstered as the furniture, beings without definite pursuits or permanent relations, who drifted on a languid tide of curiosity from restaurant to concert hall, from palm garden to music room." "Somewhere behind them," Wharton continued, "in the background of their lives, there was doubtless a real past, peopled by real human activities" (*House of Mirth* 274). For John C. Van Dyke, however, the past that was most interesting was not that of his noble family line or of the social lineages that stratified his New York world. The past that interested Van Dyke was geologic and Paleolithic. It was best revealed in "the weird solitude, the great silence, the grim desolation" of the desert. This past and this aesthetic, Van Dyke believed, would cure "the premonitory symptoms of racial decay" (13) he saw around him. He was a Turnerite, through and through.

The American deserts sharpened Van Dyke's diagnosis of what ailed his capricious upper-class culture. He discovered the desert to be Darwinian and antiprogressive, yet uniquely American. It threw down a new challenge before Van Dyke's Anglo-Saxon culture: stay fit, adapt, and survive.

But it did so on old American mythic terms. It still beckoned west. It still argued that European traditions were exhausted (and were now creeping into upper-class American traditions and enervating them as well). It still claimed that only an *American* place could revive them.

Throughout *The Desert*, Van Dyke finds that the arid land reveals "a war of elements and a struggle for existence." All around him he sees Darwinian strife—"barb and thorn," "jaw and paw," "beak and talon," "sting and poison." Even the slow-moving Colorado impresses him in "its fierce struggle with the encompassing rock" (63). Everything is at war in Van Dyke's desert, and the animals and plants he finds there, are "marvelous engines of resistance" (133).

It is peculiar that, in Van Dyke's mind, this elemental struggle showed that "nature . . . wishes to maintain the *status quo*" (132). While many Americans of his day thought of nature as progressive, as designing species with ever-greater efficiency and purpose, Van Dyke was not a believer. For him the desert showed that nature "breaks the conqueror on his shield."

The desert also bore witness to the fact that American progress was invariably made at the expense of her natural resources. The wild landscape and frontier that were supposed to revivify European cultures were routinely sacrificed to the ideal of progress. It was oil and coal and timber and copper that the West had provided in place of Jefferson's homesteads and villages. To Van Dyke, American life at the end of the nineteenth century was totally focused on efforts "to get the dollar, and if there is any money in cutting the throat of Beauty, why, by all means, cut her throat" (60). The desert was simply the last stop on the coal train of progress:

> It is not necessary to dig up ancient history; for have we not seen, here in California and Oregon, in our own time, the destruction of the fairest valleys the sun ever shone upon by placer and hydraulic mining? Have we not seen in Minnesota and Wisconsin the mightiest forest . . . slashed to pieces by the broadax and turned into a waste of treestumps and fallen timber? . . . Men must have coal though they ruin the valleys and blacken the streams of Pennsylvania, they must have oil though they disfigure half of Ohio and Indiana, they must have copper if they wreck all of the mountains of Montana and Arizona, and they must have gold though they blow Alaska into the Bering Sea. (60–61)

The human, built environment that followed from such exploitation was predictably awful, consisting of little more than "weeds, wire fences, oil-derrick, board shanties and board towns."

Yet even as the desert—the last frontier of the "practical men"—stood ravaged, its desolate aridity inspired Van Dyke to hope that there, progress might finally founder. "Reclaiming a waste may not be so easy as breaking a prairie or cutting down a forest," Van Dyke happily predicted, "and Nature will not always be driven from her purpose."

The only thing that threatened the desert's ultimate triumph over American greed and destruction was irrigation—another "practical" swindle, in Van Dyke's opinion. He noted that "a great company has been formed to turn the Colorado River into the sands, to reclaim this desert basin, and make it blossom as the rose," but mockingly added, it would be by these means "fitted for homesteads, ready for the settler who ever remains unsettled" (57).

Part conservationism, part primitivism, and thoroughly antiprogressive and antiyeoman, Van Dyke's attack on irrigation exposes the fundamental cultural anxiety beneath his newfound appreciation of the desert. Progress will domesticate the desert's beauty, replacing it with some latter-day Hudson River aesthetic—banal, ersatz landscapes of florid sunsets and picturesque cowboys. Van Dyke really hated the western art that had flourished under the progressive vision. He begged off to a journal editor who had requested a commentary on Frederick Remington's "The Bucking Bronco," instead recommending Theodore Roosevelt as someone who could write "half a page of more interesting reading on the subject" (82). Such anecdotes reflect the aesthetic ideals that play into Van Dyke's celebration of the desert as the necessary corrective to the cloying nineteenth-century, East-Coast landscape tradition of painters like Thomas Cole, leader of the Hudson River School. "One begins by admiring the Hudson-River landscape," Van Dyke observed, "and ends by loving the desolation of the Sahara" (x).

Of course, Van Dyke is not really interested in the African Sahara. From the preface onward, he makes it clear that it is the aesthetics of the *American* desert that will heal the moral lapses in the national character. "We have often heard of 'Sunny Italy' of the 'clear light' of Egypt," Van Dyke remarks, "but believe me, there is no sunlight there compared with that which falls upon the upper peaks of the Sierra Madre of the uninhabitable wastes of the Colorado Desert. Pure sunlight requires for its existence pure air, and the Old World has little of it left" (ix). To Van Dyke, European sunshine is tainted by a "chemical color" and is not worthy of comparison with the newly discovered "gold and purple and burning crimson of this new world" (x).

Van Dyke had some difficulty, however, in finding a piece of the American desert to claim as his own. Utah and Death Valley had already been done to death, with tales of Indian ambush and settler parties dying of thirst. Same for the Colorado River's canyon country. Nevada? Nevada was the stuff of mining stories and roaring camps. Even Van Dyke's brother had gotten to the Mojave Desert first, writing articles for the popular regionalist magazine, *The Land of Sunshine*. Van Dyke settled on the Imperial Valley, and especially its below-sea-level center, the Salton Sink, as the set piece for his theory of a modern American art based on desert optics in their purest form. Van Dyke renamed the Salton Basin "the Big Bowl," and in its depths mixed up a palette of myth and modernism.

Besides its austerity, the Imperial Valley had other things to recommend it. It was on the Mexican border, a legendary locale of Spanish expeditions, conquests, and outlawry. It was skirted by the greatest river of the West, the Colorado, which was itself the stuff of legend and conquest. Even better, no one in eastern American was yet familiar with its southernmost reaches, near its termination in the Gulf of California. It was also under immanent threat of being reclaimed by irrigation, its beauty poised on the knife-edge of progress. At any moment, it might be domesticated by capitalism.

In retrospect, Van Dyke seems to have chosen well. His book went through fourteen editions in the first three decades of the century. And while his story is shot through with Darwinian struggle, antiprogressive skepticism, and nationalist sentiment, it was not these things that attracted readers and made them see the arid West anew. It was the color Van Dyke discovered there. It was the way he described the play of shadow on a canyon rim at twilight and the shimmering of a mirage at midday.

The Desert opens with a black-and-white photograph of an arid mountain; its caption introduces a theme that will be repeated throughout the book: "silence and desolation" (see figure 5). The figure and title set the barren backdrop for the narrator's heroic aesthetic exploits.

They also initiate a thematic tension—between the desert's silence and the narrator's verbose lectures—that will suspend the rest of the book between tragedy and comedy, between dejection and exhilaration. At times, the desert's river boundary, the Colorado, is "almost tragic in its swift transitions" (63). Here is the desert of Darwin, of the war for survival, of crisp demarcations between light and dark, good and evil. At other times, however, the book invokes a gentler, almost pastoral vision. It charts the course of a day, beginning in the morning with a hike up to the top of a desert peak and ending on the Coastal Range of the Pacific, looking back across the desert at the coming dusk. At such moments, Van Dyke transforms the desert into a middle landscape, a place to escape both the uncivilized wilderness and the overcivilized city.

There are similar tensions at play in the narrator himself. Sometimes he is a cowboy, at other times a scientist or aesthete. Take, for example, his description of a night spent under the desert stars:

> Lying down there in the sands of the desert, alone and at night, with a saddle for your pillow, and your eyes staring upward at the stars, how incomprehensible it all seems! The immensity and the mystery are appalling; and yet how these very features attract the thought and draw the curiosity of man. In the presence of the unattainable and the insurmountable we keep sending a hope, a doubt, a query, up through the realms of air to Saturn's throne.... Around us stretches the great sand-wrapped desert whose mystery no man knows.... What is it that draws us to the boundless and the fathomless? (106)

Rational, yet manly and adventurous, the narrator of *The Desert* casts a scornful glance back at the failures of his romantic predecessors: "Scott, Byron, Hugo,—not one of the old romanticists ever knew Nature except as in some strained way symbolic of human happiness or misery" (211). He has harsh words as well for the scientists of the previous generation: "They were impressed at first only with the large and more apparent beauties of the world—the Alps, the Niagras, the Grand Canyons, the panoramic views from mountain-tops. They never would have tolerated the desert for a moment" (211).

To compensate for such failures, Van Dyke goes out of his way to ensure his book is an antipanoramic, antitranscendence story. Although it opens like any other romantic story of mountain climbing, Van Dyke's ascent is different. The desert slopes are known as "Lost Mountains," and they appear only as a "surviving remnant . . . of some noble range." It is their antiquity rather than their elevation that fascinates Van Dyke. It is also their mystery. Like Anza, he discovers that though they seem close by, constant riding brings them no closer. They become an ideal image of the elusiveness of truth and transcendence in this "land of illusion and thin air." Precluded from the possibility of transcendence, Van Dyke is left with gravel and what he calls "the chief glory of the desert, . . . its broad blaze of omnipresent light." The key phrase in his description of the approach to the Lost Mountains becomes "deception," as the traditional spatial organization of nature is distorted by desert shadows and desert distances: "You can be deceived by the nearness of things quite as often as by their remoteness."

FIGURE 5. *Silence and Desolation*, from *The Desert* (1901). Courtesy of the Edward E. Ayer Collection, The Newberry Library, Chicago.

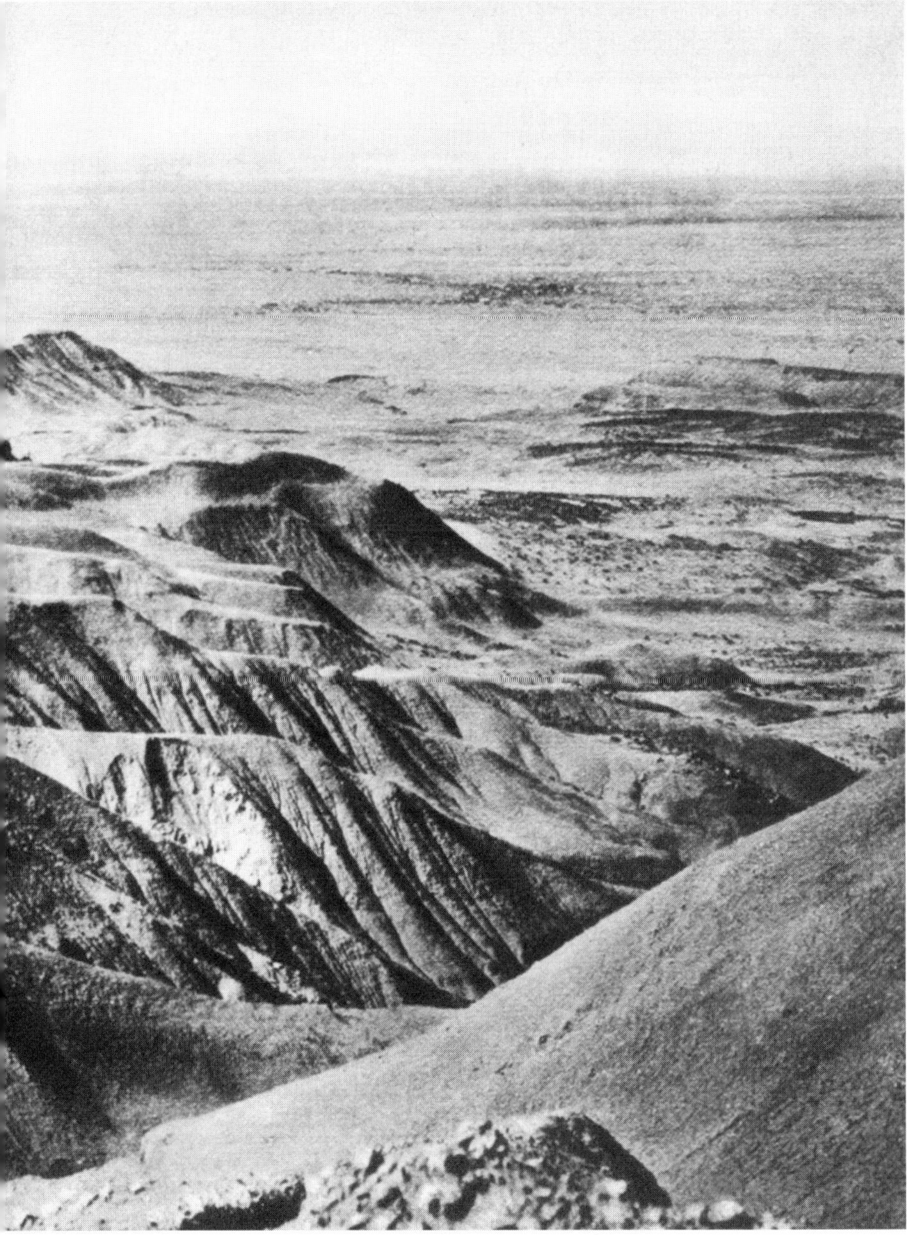

Van Dyke does eventually attain the summit, however, and finds it anticlimactically flat. Amid its rubble-strewn expanse, he discerns a horseshoe-shaped stone enclosure, the remains of "a once fortified camp." He can't help but ponder the motivations of the ancient desert dwellers who built it. Did they love the desert light as much as he does? Why had they chosen such an arid, desolate mountaintop to build their dwelling place? Van Dyke concludes that they must have "loved the open country." But did they love "the view"?

Ultimately, Van Dyke decides, "it is not likely that the tribe ever chose this abiding place for its scenery." After all, he reasons, "the peons and Indians in Sonora cannot see the pinks and purples in the mountain shadows at sunset. They are astonished at your question for they see nothing but mountains." In the end he pronounces his verdict: "A wealth of color and atmospheric effect was wasted upon the aboriginal retina."

Van Dyke considers his own ability to mine color and beauty from the desert to be the result of racial evolution. Perversely labeling his highly developed aesthetic taste a "premonitory symptom of racial decay," he explains that "a sensitive feeling for sound, or form, or color" is the result of the modern-day Anglo-Saxon's "impressionable nervous organization." Such delicate sensibilities could not belong to "the man with the hoe much less to the man with the bow." Neither Jefferson's yeoman farmer nor the native hunter is psychologically suited for desert appreciation.

Referring to the original inhabitants of the Lost Mountains as the "brown skins" and "suntanned people," Van Dyke euphemistically reduces them to mere colors in the landscape, much like the pinks, terra cottas, and oranges he admires from the mountaintop. While they "never gave thought to masses or horizontal lines, or paradoxes," these are the resources that this latter-day conquistador wishes to mine in lieu of the gold and silver the "practical men" of his generation seek there.

Thus the book's opening ascent of the desert mountain provides John Van Dyke with several things unavailable to nineteenth-century romantic mountain climbers. He gains cultural distance from both Native peoples and the sodbusters of the Anglo American West. He attains an aristocratic bearing in that he is consigned neither, like the Indian, to the bow, nor, like the yeoman, to a ploughshare. He gains his own generation's—largely imaginary—past and evolves beyond it. He becomes free, moreover, from the capitalist engine that demanded real golds and silvers. Finally, he acquires for himself the cultural capital accrued by the Spanish, the Europeans who encountered this land before him, by letting his mind wander a little further into the past on his descent from the mountain summit:

> As I ride off across the plain to the east the thought of the heroism, the self-abnegation, the undying faith of those followers of Loyola and Xavier who came into this waste so many years ago.... The Padres were men of soul, unshrinking faith, and perseverance almost unparalleled in the annals of history. The accomplishments of Columbus, of Cortez, of Coronado were great; but what of those who first ventured out upon these sands and erected missions almost in the heart of the desert, who single-handed coped with dangers from man and nature. Has not the sign of the cross cast more men in heroic mould than ever the glitter of the crown or the flash of the sword? (20–21)

The god Van Dyke worships, however, is of quite another cast. Somewhere between an imagined native natural religion and an equally romanticized Catholicism, he finds himself overwhelmed by the vast, abstracted shapes that the mountain peak has opened to his view:

> There is simplicity about large masses—simplicity in breadth, space, and distance—that is inviting and ennobling. And there is something restful about the horizontal line ... the weird solitude, the great silence, the grim desolation, are the very things with which every desert wanderer eventually falls in love. (19)

As he embraces this modern, minimalist eternal present, he realizes that the view of the desert from the mountain does not yield "transcendence" but rather perspectival distance, a big-picture ability to shake out the great masses and large forms that make up desert beauty. It is the enormity of shape and open space that is important, and the process of ascent is valuable only insofar as it simplifies and abstracts these from the historical whole of abandoned mountaintop encampment and dusty Pueblo mission.

The next chapter of Van Dyke's book, "The Make of the Desert," explores these shapes and spaces more closely, describing the real-world environmental forces behind them. Aridity; sudden, destructive cloudbursts; scouring winds; eternal heat—all contribute to the desert's "poetry of ... wide-spread chaos." They also indemnify it from Hudson River sentimentality: "There is not a thing about it that is 'pretty,' and not a spot upon it that is 'picturesque' in any Berkshire-Valley sense. The shadows of foliage, the drift of clouds, the fall of rain upon leaves, the sound of running waters—all the gentler qualities of nature that minor poets love to juggle with—are missing on the desert" (25). Though the desert remains an "empire," in metaphor at least, it is an empire governed by an elemental and ruthless sovereign—the sun.

Meandering from desert mountain to desert elements, Van Dyke arrives finally at two central chapters that sharpen to a fine edge the abstract and elemental aesthetic he has been seeking. It is in the Lower Colorado's Salton Sink, the below-sea-level salt flat at the valley's center, and in the Colorado River itself, that he finds the purest desert aesthetic. The downward flow of his narrative into the "Bottom of the Bowl" inverts the traditional romantic ascent to plumb the depths of "the hottest place to be found anywhere on the American deserts." It moves then to "The Silent River," his antiromantic paean to the lower reaches of the Colorado.

"The Bottom of the Bowl" begins with the prehistory of the Salton Sink—with the receding of Lake Cahuilla, the seasonal flooding of the New River arroyo, and the resiliency of the native people living there. In Van Dyke's portrait, the *pure* desert embodied by the drying lakebed seems almost like an ancient sea creature exposed to light for the first time. With a "surface too salt and alkaline to allow of much vegetation," it is all shape and stratum, space and light. The dunes around the Salton Basin are sheer sculpture in the shifting daylight:

> The desert sand is finer than snow, and its curves and arches, as it builds its succession of drifts out and over an arroyo, are as graceful as the lines of running water. The dunes are always rhythmical and flowing in their forms; and for color the desert has nothing that surpasses them. In the early morning, before the sun is up, they are air-blue, reflecting the sky overhead; at noon they are pale lines of dazzling orange-colored light, waving and undulating in the heated air, at sunset they are often flooded with a rose or mauve color; under a blue moonlight they shine white as icebergs in the northern seas. (53)

Even animals are reluctant to linger in this stark landscape. Their tracks suggest the purposiveness of those who dare to venture in: "They all run in straight trails, showing the animals to be crossing the basin to the mountains, not prowling or hunting" (54).

Perhaps even more important than the basin's austerity is the way it is given to subtle optical illusions like the mirage, the result of light refracting off the shimmering sand and salt to blend with air and color. The Salton Basin solves the dilemma faced by the modern painter: "[How] to get on with the least possible form and to suggest everything by tones of color, shades of light, drifts of air." Because "the landscape that is the simplest in form and the finest in color is by all odds the most beautiful," the Big Bowl is declared a "thing of beauty instead of a dreary hollow in the hills."

Threatening the Big Bowl's proffer of salvation to the modern artist are the plans of the practical men who wish to see it irrigated and blooming. Water "is to be brought down to the basin by the old channel of the New River . . . to be distributed over the tracts by irrigating ditches." Seeing nothing but aesthetic doom in this promise of progress, Van Dyke pleads for preservation in much the same language that his contemporaries were using for the establishment of the great national parks: "The deserts should never be reclaimed. They are the breathing spaces of the West and should be preserved forever." Realizing that commercial exploitation of this last piece of the frontier is inevitable, he takes solace in his belief that the same elemental forces that make this desert beautiful will ultimately deliver it from progress: "When man is gone, the sand and the heat will come back to the desert. The desolation of the kingdom will live again, and down in the Bottom of the bowl the opalescent mirage will waver skyward on wings of light, serene in its solitude, though no human eye sees nor human tongue speaks its loveliness" (62).

Van Dyke turns his attention from this austere space of pure silence and desolation at the center of the Imperial Valley, to its eastern border, the Colorado River, which "acts as a catch-basin for all the running color of the desert" (68). Some of his best descriptive writing may be found here, caressing the slow-moving water with a matching deliberateness of detail. Playing on the Spanish meaning of the word *colorado*—the hot red of chilies—Van Dyke explicates the river's redness as, by turns, a "savage" tide, a "trail of blood," a "red hue of decay." With a quick verbal turn, he domesticates it, making it seem less threatening: "The Colorado is a red river but not a scarlet one" (67). That is, the river is no scarlet lady, no figure of dime novel romance. With another sleight of hand, he orientalizes it, and we see it surging with the red tints of Asian ceramics, the "sang-de-boef" colors Van Dyke loves. It is a mystery, an object d'art, a trifle to be turned, with satisfaction, over and over in the mind.

At its delta, where it slouches into the Sea of Cortez, the river's quiet seems primeval:

> There are no towns or roads or people by those shores, there are no ships upon those seas, there are no dust and smoke of factories in those skies. The Indians are there as undisturbed as in the days of Coronado, and the white man is coming but

> has not yet arrived. The sun still shines on unknown bays and unexplored peaks. Therefore is there silence—something of the hush of the deserts and the river that flows between. (76)

In an America of urban encroachment and immigrant masses, here is shelter in the last stretches of the Colorado through the Imperial Valley. The distant past beckons.

Having established the boundaries of this most perfect stretch of minimalist scenery, *The Desert* then opens up into the pure elements of impressionism. In "Light, Air, and Color," "Desert Sky and Clouds," and "Illusions," Van Dyke details the optical characteristics of what he calls the desert's "local color." One is struck, when reading these chapters, by Van Dyke's fascination with the physics of the desert. He talks about angles and refraction, about density and distance. It soon becomes clear that he is exploring what art historian Jonathan Crary has called the "techniques of the observer."

Van Dyke's celebration of the desert's beauty came at the climax of a revolution in Euro American seeing and representing that placed the human mind, the individual subject, at the center of aesthetic appreciation and artistic production. Across American culture during the nineteenth century, there was an explosion of interest in the nature of the observer of aesthetic objects, so much so that scientists and artists (as well as toymakers and entertainers) became fascinated with optical illusions, kaleidoscopes, afterimages, and the like. The eighteenth century's model of optical perfection, the camera obscura, a darkened chamber that projected an image of an outdoor scene onto a table or screen for the stable enjoyment of an observer inside, gave way to visual experiments that focused on the fallibility, mobility, and changeability of the observer. For John C. Van Dyke, the whole desert floor served as an optical laboratory, challenging all the theories of light and color that underwrote nineteenth-century academic painting.

In "Illusions" Van Dyke revels in the desert's power to confound ordinary human senses. Here, "bodies fail to detach themselves one from another, foreshortening is abnormal, the planes of landscape are flattened out of shape or telescoped, objects are huddled together or superimposed one upon another" (113). The desert also defeats the expectation of a unitary light source, so central to traditional painting. The rocks and vegetation make false shadows, so that there are hundreds of contradictory signals—is the sun setting or rising? The most inspiring light show of all is the mirage, and the Lower Colorado is particularly prone to them because of its flatness and distances. Using optical theory, Van Dyke explains how the mind's engagement with the desert invents these wishful lakes of shimmering light by virtue of its slavish adherence to the laws of physics: "Light comes to us in comparatively straight rays. The mind, therefore, has formulated a law that we see only by straight rays. In the case of the mirage the light comes to us on curved, bent or angular rays. The eyes recognize this, but the mind refuses to believe it and hence is deceived." At times, the mirage appears simply as an ever-receding lake; at others, it creates mountains looming over the horizon like floating islands, or even, "mountains hanging peak downward from the sky."

Effects like these would likely have inspired fear and dread in the imaginations of eighteenth-century viewers. They delight Van Dyke, who finds that the "kaleidoscopic changes keep the fancy moving at a pretty pace." The mirage contains within itself both the moderns' love of fast-paced imagery and excitement and the antimodernist triumph over technology: "You cannot see it clear-cut and well-defined, and the snap-shot of your camera does not catch it at all." The willingness of the observer to give himself over to the illusion of the mirage even when he knows its physics becomes one of *The Desert*'s central points—the modern American must turn away from realism and towards the imagination, but they must be prepared to encounter something "elemental," something equally unromantic.

To put the finishing touches on his own version of the desert aesthetic, Van Dyke ends his book with one final ascent, this time of the Pacific coastal range to the West of the Imperial Valley. Observing that "the desert does not give up dominion easily," (217) Van Dyke turns his back on the Pacific to consider the desert's final lesson. Below him, the terra cotta granite of the Big Bowl shows through the chaparral, and the small plots of cultivated land appear insignificant in proportion to the desert's vastness. The view of the desert from atop the Pacific Range reassures Van Dyke, for the sprinkling of towns and farms convinces him that "cultivated conditions are maintained only at the price of eternal vigilance" (228). As an elemental force, the desert provides something Van Dyke's wandering generation lacks, but even the prophet of the arid West cannot be sure whether "this great expanse of sand and rock is the beginning or the end" of civilization and progress (231). The stretches of the Lower Colorado "are beautiful themselves and good to look upon whether they be life or death" (232). Theirs is a tactile truth that offers the modern observer at the dawn of the twentieth century the kind of felt experience that academic painting and photography could not. On the book's final page, as he contemplates the "dusk gathering on the desert's face," Van Dyke is left with an overwhelming sense of "mystery—that haunting sense of the unknown" (233).

FIGURE 6. Emma Augusta Ayer, *Desolation on the Yuma Desert*. Courtesy of the Edward E. Ayer Collection, The Newberry Library, Chicago.

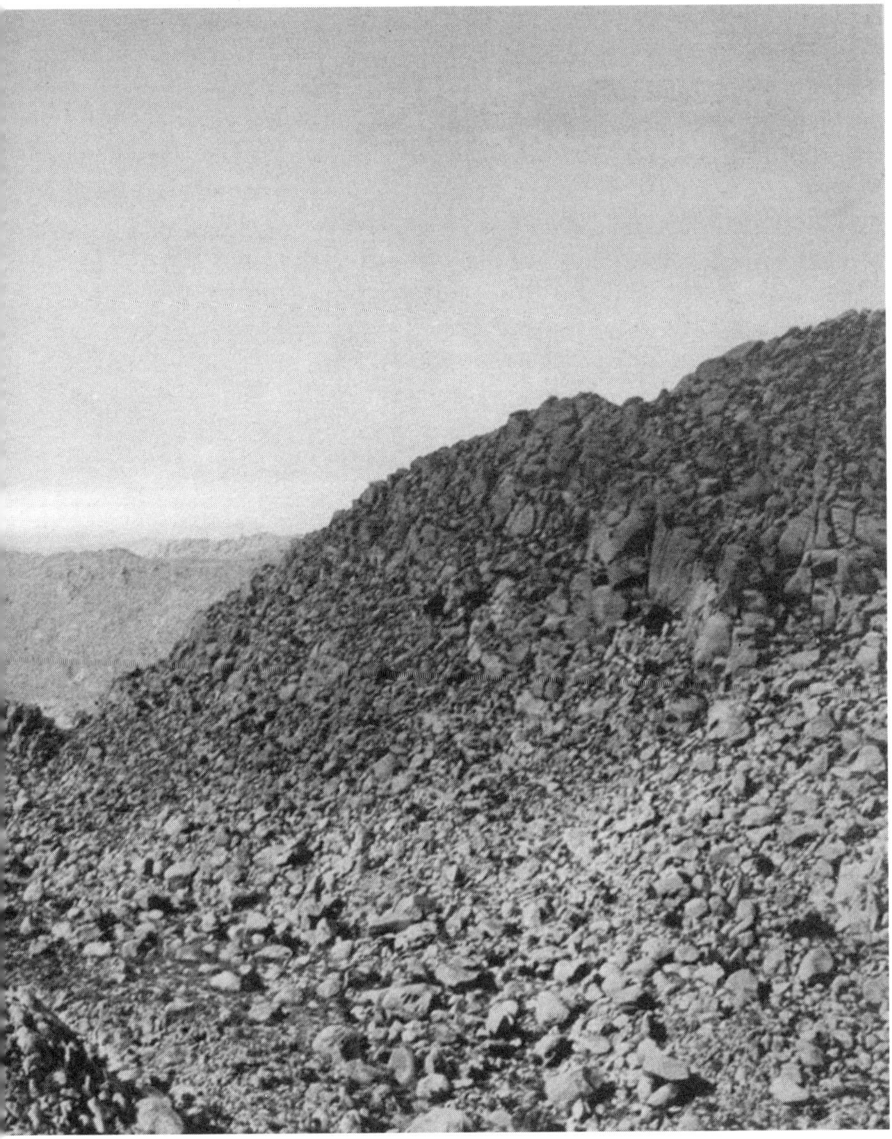

Van Dyke's story of the Lower Colorado fired the imaginations of many Americans. Edward Ayer, founder of the Field Museum in Chicago, was among them. Ayer and his wife bought the 1918 edition of *The Desert* and carried it with them on a trip to the Southwest that same year. When they returned, they had the book rebound to include their own personal snapshots as illustrations for Van Dyke's words. Where Van Dyke begins his description of the Big Bowl, the Ayer's edition inserts a photograph of the road to the Imperial Valley with the hand-lettered caption, "Desolation on the Yuma Desert" (see figure 6). In his manuscript memoir of the trip, Edward Ayer tells how at one point in the journey he and his wife returned to their hotel to find John C. Van Dyke himself sitting in the lobby. He was, Ayer explained, the "gentleman Mrs. Ayer and I are more indebted to than any other in the world for our knowledge of the desert." Ayer confesses that while he had visited this same desert thirty years earlier, he had no "idea of its grandeur and beauty" until he read Van Dyke. Such was the power of Van Dyke's story of place.

The Desert spawned a new storytelling tradition across the West. This tradition, which included works ranging from Mary Austin's *The Land of Little Rain* (1906) to Edward Abbey's *Desert Solitaire* (1968), turned the story of the arid Great Basin into a quest for aesthetic independence. It attracted people by the thousands to landscapes their grandparents would have been horrified to see outside their parlor windows. Yet the very aesthetic independence that Van Dyke thought would save America from its Progressive fever to tame the western landscape actually played into the hands of the developers he sought to quash. Van Dyke's gunmetal mountains and chalk white sand flats served as a sublime background for an emerging storytelling foreground of picturesque sunlit irrigated fields and pastures of plenty. This rival set of tales also claimed that American inspiration could be regained in the arid West, but it argued that engineering, not art, would be the source of the cultural reawakening. In these storytellers' fables of desert reclamation, the land was crying out for water and virtuous capitalist financiers were heeding its call. By 1918, Van Dyke's Big Bowl, the crucible of light and shadow, color and vision that was to save America's aesthetic soul, was under more than thirty feet of inland sea.

3 "Water is King, Here is its Kingdom"

| During the nineteenth century, Californians' thirst for water was second only to their thirst for gold. By the first decades of the twentieth, it outstripped all other desires put together. Californians needed water and they needed it now. So they dammed up Hetch Hetchy and piped the Owens River down to Los Angeles.

My valley's role in the rush for water is nearly forgotten today. But in 1911, everybody in America was talking about it. This was because in the Imperial Valley, the delivery of water went hand in hand with the arrival of professional storytelling. The greatest apologist for the valley's irrigation project was a short-term resident, Harold Bell Wright, America's most popular novelist in the first decade of the twentieth century. Wright had moved to the valley in 1908 for his health, having already made his name as one of America's foremost regionalist writers. An earlier Wright novel, *The Shepard of the Hills* (1900), had put the Ozarks on the map of the national imagination and turned it into a desirable destination for tourists and vacationers. After raising horses in the Imperial Valley for a short time, Wright became fascinated with the notion of desert reclamation and, with the encouragement of local boosters, turned his attention to writing a novel centered on the Imperial Valley's water project. The resulting work, *The Winning of Barbara Worth* (1911), is a romance that dramatizes the struggle between the two great forces in America's westward expansion. "Without water," Wright's hero observes, "the desert was worthless.... Without Capital," he continues, "the water could not be had."

In 1925, Samuel Goldwyn of MGM offered Wright $125,000 for the rights to *The Winning of Barbara Worth*, calling the reclamation of the desert "drama itself." The film version was screened the following year in Los Angeles for a group of movie stars and conferees assembled to discuss the "winning of the West." Wright's story provided the keynote for a conference whose agenda was to "make the desert 'blossom as a rose' and reclaim approx. 1.5 million worth of land now useless." Where John C. Van Dyke heard only profound silence in the Imperial Valley, Barbara Worth, Wright's eponymous heroine, hears the desert "calling—calling; waiting—waiting for someone." That someone is her father, the benevolent capitalist hero of the story, who eventually finances the great water project that makes the Big Bowl *imperial*.

While Van Dyke had seen it coming, he could not have known when he took that last long look at the Salton Basin in 1901 that it would happen so fast. Within four years, the Salton Sink was inundated by the Colorado River. In the spring of 1905, due partly to natural forces and partly to errors of human engineering, the Colorado broke free of its channel, turning north to fill the low lying lands of the Imperial Valley. Van Dyke's arid expanse of cosmic solitude was transformed into an inland saltwater sea of biblical proportions.

In truth, a time-immemorial, static desert ecosystem had always been a figment of Van Dyke's imagination. For hundreds of years, the Colorado, which sits almost two hundred feet above the valley floor, had bolted its banks during the summer flood season, engulfing the lower, flatter land of the Imperial Valley. This cyclical flooding inspired the valley's first American settlers and tourists to give often-dry places incongruous names like Blue Lake, Pelican, and Swimming Hole.

It also deposited a rich layer of alluvial soil into this below-sea-level trench, in some places several hundred feet in depth. With a yearlong growing season, and ultra-fecund (if arid) earth, the Big Bowl soon had restless entrepreneurs eyeing it with speculative lust. If the seasonal flooding could be tamed, if water could be brought to fields year round, one booster observed in 1910, "the story of the achievements of the pioneers of Imperial Valley will some day be recognized as the narrative of one of the most important stages in the constructions of an empire in the Southwest, the glory of which the keenest visioned of us all can now but dimly see" (Howe and Hall 5).

Throughout the nineteenth century, plans had been made to transform "this waste . . . into a productive territory" (Howe and Hall 23). They had all been brought to ground by technical and capital limitations. It wasn't until the 1890s, when the growth of Los Angeles spurred railroad expansion into the desert reaches of Southern California, that capital could be enticed to this last western frontier and the early pioneers' dreams of an "imperial" desert valley could be realized.

The story of the transformation of Van Dyke's arid Big Bowl into the irrigated Imperial Valley begins with a young engineer, Charles Robinson Rockwood, who accidentally discovered the agricultural potential of the Lower Colorado Desert while surveying Mexican land south of Yuma, Arizona, for a Denver land promoter named John Beatty. Another member of the fin de siècle restless generation, Rockwood had roamed the West for a number of years after graduating with an engineering degree from the University of Michigan. He worked for the Southern Pacific Railroad and the U.S. Geological Survey before striking out on Beatty's venture in 1892.

When he first recognized the singular combination of gifts that centuries of time and tricks of geography had given the Salton Basin—rich soil, a long growing season, and water that seemed to *want* to flow there—Rockwood was beside himself. Dropping Beatty's plan to survey the Sonoran lands to the southeast, he hastily scribbled his observations into a private journal. Someday, he predicted, "one of the most meritorious irrigation projects in the country would be bringing together the land of the Colorado Desert and the water of the Colorado River" (Tout 29).

But vision alone was not enough to make the Salton Basin imperial. It required cash, and lots of it. Thus Rockwood the engineer became Rockwood the pitchman. He would spend the next several years combing the ranks of his restless generation for prospective investors. The world of land speculation in California at the end of the nineteenth century was a snarl of individual holdings and development companies, shady investors and loud-mouthed admen. As Rockwood angled for capital to secure land rights and easements on both sides of the border, his pristine vision became more and more entangled in what the novelist Frank Norris called the "octopus" of finance capitalism.

Soon, Rockwood's personal quest had been auctioned off to a group of businessmen who felt their role in this unique microcosm was "to save the land from itself" (Wright 136). There was Anthony H. Heber from Chicago, an agent for the Kern County Corporation, which was already knee-deep in business dealings that mixed reclamation and investment in central California. A fastidious man, the pince-nez wearing Heber looked like a cross between Woodrow Wilson and the timid bank manager in a TV western. After hearing Rockwood's plans, Heber became a tireless promoter of the reclamation project. When the federal government threatened to intervene in the valley's development, Heber rushed to Washington to deliver a strident ultimatum: "It is my earnest wish to worship at our own altar, and to receive the blessing from the shine of our own Government, but if such permission is not given, we shall be compelled to worship elsewhere" (Tout 99). The implication of Heber's classically American blend of Christian millennialism and capitalist rhetoric was simply this: he and his fellow investors would look to Mexico for water rights if the United States became a hindrance to their plans.

Another major player in the project was Don Guillermo Andrade, a Mexican gentleman born in Hermosillo in 1829 and educated in Europe. After running a sugar plantation in good old nineteenth-century colonial fashion, Andrade got caught up in the restless zeitgeist of the times and came to California in 1879 in search of gold. In San Francisco, Andrade established the first steamship line working the West Coast of Mexico from Manzanillo and Guaymas. He soon earned enough money and influence to secure a thirty-five-thousand-acre tract of land in Baja California just south of the Imperial Valley. His holdings stretched from the Gulf of California to the mouth of the Colorado. By the time Rockwood set out to dredge a channel through Mexico, Andrade controlled upward of 100,000 acres of land and also had the ear of authorities in Mexico City.

Finally, there was Harry Chandler, publisher of the *Los Angeles Times*, and perhaps the most powerful man in the Southwest in the first decades of the twentieth century. During the reclamation of the Imperial Valley, Chandler would acquire 860,000 acres of Mexican land fed by the Colorado.

Brought together by a combination of investment and vision, greed and guile, these men founded the California Development Company (CDC) in 1896. The CDC immediately began to sell "land script" investments in its plans for drawing water out of the Colorado to irrigate the desert. Rockwood and Heber crisscrossed the continent many times over the next three years, even booking passage to England and the Continent in search of more investors.

But as the progressive new century dawned, they came up broke. Heber even had to pawn his wife's jewelry for $125 just to keep the project afloat.

It would take a canal builder with international experience and a real personal fortune to turn the CDC around. That man was Canadian engineer George Chaffey, who was renowned for the irrigation system he had designed to water his Rancho Cucamonga farm. When his son warned him that the Imperial Valley scheme, though technically feasible as an engineering effort, was deeply flawed as a business proposition, Chaffey reportedly said, "Let me do one more big thing before I die." In April 1900, the California Development Company contracted with Chaffey to build the irrigation project Rockwood had envisioned. During the twenty-two months Chaffey oversaw the project, four hundred miles of canals and laterals were built, and in May 1901, the Colorado began flowing into the valley.

By February 1905, Chaffey's work was overmatched by mother nature, and as the Colorado rushed unimpeded to fill the Salton sink and to inundate the fledgling agricultural lands of the valley, it seemed as though Rockwell's dream would join a growing list of overreaching progressivist engineering failures. Like the collapse of William Mulholand's St. Francis dam in the San Francisquito Valley twenty-three years later—an engineering blunder that cost 450 lives and exposed the rotten political core of the Los Angeles aqueduct project—the California Development Company's gamble looked to become a very different story from the one Rockwell had imagined. The new version detailed how self-interest was insufficient to manage natural resources and protect the dreams of working men and women.

Harold Bell Wright arrived in the Imperial Valley just after this spectacular reclamation blunder. Before he moved on, he had produced a novel that itself reclaimed the sordid history of the valley's first irrigation efforts and turned them into the stuff of legend. It was a magical transformation that saved the valley's image for future settlers and investors and was in many ways the culmination of Wright's writing career.

The man who wrote the Imperial Valley's first best seller was a drifter with the soul of an evangelist. He never lived in a city, and all his life preferred to reside miles from the nearest town in isolated ranchos of his own design. Everyone who met him thought he looked like Abraham Lincoln.

Perhaps the resemblance was due to the fact that he too was a self-educated man who had lived a hard life. At age twelve, when his mother died, the boy was simply sent out on his own by his drunken father. After drifting around, painting houses and riding the rails, Wright was called to Christian fellowship when a visiting evangelist convinced him to enter the Disciples'

Hiram College in Ohio. His education was short-lived. After only two years at Hiram, Wright left the school, forced out by ill heath and a nagging feeling that his "call" was to work, not to the ordained ministry.

For a while, he pounded rocks at a quarry while writing in the evening, convinced that such "applied Christianity" would be both useful and saving. But Wright had a streak of Huck Finn in him too. He soon abandoned the quarry to float a homemade canoe down the Mississippi. His canoe took him as far as the Ozarks, where he was called by a congregation to preach.

For the next ten years, Wright shepherded flocks at the Pierce City Christian Church in the Ozarks and the Christian Church of Pittsburg, Kansas. His big break as a writer came in 1901 when he met Elsberry W. Reynolds, a salesman for a mail-order Christian bookselling firm. Reynolds thought Wright a first-rate storyteller, and even though his outfit, the Book Supply Company, was in the business of selling—not publishing—tracts and didactic novels, Reynolds convinced his boss to give Wright a try as a novelist. The Book Supply Company brought out *That Printer of Udell's*, Wright's first book, in 1903. It was the story of an itinerant printer and his quest for a useful, Christian life. Like all his subsequent books, *That Printer* was intended, as Wright put it, "to build an influence for right living."

Returning to the Ozarks, Wright soon completed *The Shepard of the Hills*, his second and most famous novel. It was a potboiler—a moral fable about a citified protagonist who goes to the Ozarks and falls in love with a local girl. When she discovers she is pregnant, he abandons her to seek his fortune elsewhere. She dies in childbirth, and the tragedy is complete. Aside from its moral appeal, *The Shepard of the Hills* was popular for its regionalist depiction of life in the economically depressed but morally upright villages of the hill country, as well as for its atmospheric evocation of smoky mountains, sunsets, and russet ridges. As Wright's biographer, Lawrence V. Tagg, notes, "*The Shepard of the Hills* literally created a new geographical region, which is called 'The Shepherd of the Hills Country'" (118).

Eventually, Wright's health began to suffer from the moist Missouri mountain air, and he headed west. Arriving in Redlands, California, in 1908, Wright turned once again to preaching. It was after a morning of rousing evangelizing that Wright first met W. F. Holt, an Imperial Valley investor and booster. Holt had made a killing in the CDC's land script; the paper he purchased in 1901 had doubled in value almost overnight when Chaffey took over the water project. Like Wright, he was a transplanted Missourian. As chairman of the board of the Redlands church, Holt liked what he heard from the Lincolnesque pastor. Ever the booster, Holt talked Wright into giving up the Redlands pastorate and moving to the Salton Basin.

In the Imperial Valley, Wright started a horse breeding business on a plot of land he called Tecolote Rancho. A half-mile from the main house he built an arroweed lean-to, in which he would write some of his most successful novels—*The Calling of Dan Mathews* (1909), *The Winning of Barbara Worth* (1911), and *The Eyes of the World* (1914).

What inspired Wright to author a novel about the Imperial Valley's reclamation is unclear, but it seems that his genuine admiration for (and debt of gratitude to) Holt was an important part of it. There was also the fact that the desert appealed to his regionalist imagination and the reclamation project resonated with his Protestant work ethic. A region that had once epitomized all of the flaws of finance capitalism and progressive resource management would, in Wright's hands, be magically transformed into something "that would add immeasurably to the nation's life" (Wright 466).

In the years between the big break in Intake #3 and the publication of Wright's novel (1911), work on the reclamation of the valley had gone on apace. But the actions of the finance capitalists and land speculators threatened to sully the dream. Up and down California, the shadowy figures behind the water projects were being exposed as cheats and opportunists. Theodore Roosevelt branded them men "who in conscienceless fashion [deify] property at the expense of human rights" (Reisner 101).

Meanwhile, in the broader culture of America, "the engineer" was seeing a meteoric rise to the status of cultural hero. By 1911, engineers had become the glamorous stuff of fiction. Part of a long tradition of masculine adventure stories in America, the engineer surfaced at the end of the nineteenth century in novels like Richard Harding Davis's best seller, *Soldiers of Fortune*. Literary historian Elizabeth Ammons has characterized the mythic engineer of the period as a "titan, magician, gambler ... a celebrated national hero—who, literally, would erect a brave new century" (746). He (and it was always a *he*) epitomized the ideals of a male world of contest and achievement, and the furtherance of America's material empire in places like Panama, the Philippines, and South America.

In *Barbara Worth*, Harold Bell Wright intended to transform Rockwood, Holt, and Heber's business dealings into the stuff of myth. But how did he do it? Why did it become one of the best-selling books in the first half of the American twentieth century? The answer is that Wright gave this fad a new spin. His novel of the Imperial Valley's reclamation focused on the actions of a virtuous financier, a man who "sought to make Capital serve the race" (Wright 395).

The engineer character—called "The Seer"—fades into the background of this tale as Jefferson Worth, a good banker with the people's best interests at heart, rises to heroic stature. He is the people's champion against the moneymen who allow an impersonal market to use "man for its own ends—profit, as men use water and soil and sun and air" (Wright 395). Wright's story had the added appeal of romance. The title refers to a little orphan girl whose parents had died crossing the Colorado Desert. Jefferson Worth rescues her to raise as his own daughter. Who will win the hand and heart of the woman she will become? The tale also had action and suspense. When the shoddily constructed intakes on the Colorado River—built by the bad capitalists—collapse, will the dreams of the settlers be washed away with them?

The combination proved irresistible to the American reading public. *The Winning of Barbara Worth* placed third on the *New York Times* bestseller list for 1911. Although it slipped to sixth place the following year, it was still being devoured by enough readers in 1922 that it tied Sinclair Lewis's *Babbitt* for tenth place in the yearly rating. In 1925, MGM put it on the silver screen with a film starring Gary Cooper. Sam Goldwyn considered it his biggest picture of the year (Tagg 62). In twenty years, Rockwood's blunder had been converted into a Hollywood tale "of converting a hell of parched lands into a paradise" (Tagg 62).

Part of the story's success had to do with the undeniable appeal desert reclamation held over the American imagination. The editor of the valley's fledgling newspaper described this contemporary fascination: "Imagine how pleasing to the eye the green fields surrounded by a barren waste will be" (Howe and Hall 51). Another part of its good sales could be traced to its author's established popularity. Even before the publication of *The Winning of Barbara Worth*, Harold Bell Wright had averaged a million copies in sales for every novel he wrote. His books were even available through the Sears, Roebuck catalogue. In 1927, *Vanity Fair* listed Wright among the six most important "voices of the people" in the United States.

But some of its appeal came from the way it dealt with big ideas and contemporary cultural aspirations, rendering them understandable and appealing to a mass audience. Although Wright's opening "Acknowledgment" warns the reader that "this story is not in any way a history of this part of the Colorado Desert now known as the Imperial Valley," he admits that the "work which in the past ten years has transformed a vast desolate waste into a beautiful land of homes, cities, and farms, has been my inspiration."

The reclamation of the Imperial Valley presented Wright with a canvas broad enough to give play to huge historical forces—Capital, Good Business,

Hard Work—which he had longed to tackle on a grand scale. In fact, sometimes it seemed that Wright could only think in terms of great abstractions when he developed a fictional project. When he was writing *The Eyes of the World*, Wright didn't even name his characters until the manuscript was readied for the press. In that book, Wright told his publisher, "These characters . . . shall bear the names of the forces . . . that are so coloring and shaping the life and thought of this age" (Tagg 40). But Wright envisioned *The Winning of Barbara Worth* as something grander even than history; he called it "inspiration."

Wright had hit on a brilliant combination of storytelling and mythmaking. The book is both a page-turner and an argument about work and power, class and economics. The story is, as Sam Goldwyn put it, a tale about converting hell into paradise. You can't get much more powerful and elemental than that. But the *novel*—that combination of writerly techniques like plot, characterization, narrative point of view, and setting—works a deeper magic than Goldwyn's Hollywood pitch line would suggest.

In brief outline, the story of Barbara Worth goes like this: sometime—fifteen years before the novel's present—an engineer, a banker, an Irishman, and a Texan were surveying a California desert border country. Caught in a terrible sandstorm, the group loses its way, and very nearly succumbs to "the land of lean want, of gray death, of gaunt hunger, and torturing thirst." In foundering around, they stumble upon a lone child under the bank of a wash, not far from her mother's lifeless body. The child whines portentously, "Mamma, Barba wants a drink." It thus becomes Jefferson Worth's life mission to bring water to the girl and to the arid land that killed her parents.

The rest of the story takes place when the girl is of marrying age and the desert is ready for reclamation. Against a regionalist backdrop of "blue shadows in the canyons shading to rose and lilac and purple," and a progressivist plan to save the "land from itself," two suitors emerge to vie for her hand. One is a local boy, Abe Lee, a bastard child discovered in a mining camp and raised by the engineer (i.e., "the Seer") to become a sort of hybrid scout/surveyor. He feels both a strong bond with Barbara and the great distance between them. "It was not a distance of miles," the narrator tells us, "but of position—of circumstance" (77).

His rival for Barbara's affections is Willard Holmes, a civil engineer with a degree from an eastern university and an ancestral pedigree that includes the most powerful capitalist in the King Valley enterprise, James Greenfield. When they first meet, Holmes is taken aback by Barbara's mannish dress and lack of civilized manners. He lectures her on the importance of a noble ancestry. Barbara counters with a short manifesto of western progressivism: "The only difference between the East and the West seems to be that you *have* ancestors and that we are *going to be* ancestors.... Ancestors are to be counted as a valuable asset, but not as working capital" (131).

Through a complex series of events, all tied loosely to the real history of the Imperial Valley's reclamation, Barbara falls in love with Holmes, who is himself transformed by her and his desert experience. Barbara also learns to love her father, for whom she initially "felt ashamed... he seemed so incapable of considering anything but profit" (173). By the novel's end, "Barbara for the first time felt that she could enter fully into her father's life. She had at last seen behind his gray mask and found herself in full sympathy with him" (300).

All of this love and reconciliation is capped off by the truly implausible, but perfectly romantic, revelation that Barbara is not any old orphan, but rather James Greenfield's niece. Now a social equal, Barbara is accepted by Greenfield, who in turn embraces Jefferson Worth, his adversary through much of the novel. The man who once called Worth "an ignorant, illiterate, common boor with no breeding," now commends the novel's hero on his profound moral courage in revealing his daughter's high-status lineage at the risk of losing her to another patriarch.

The novel concludes with Holmes and Barbara in each other's arms, facing the desert, as sex and land and reclamation come together in a rush of emotion:

> "You like my Desert?" asked the young woman softly, coming closer to his side—so close that he felt her presence as clearly as he felt the presence of the spirit that lives in the desert itself.
> "Like it!" he repeated, turning toward her. "It is my desert now; mine as well as yours. Oh, Barbara! Barbara! I have learned the language of your land. Must I leave it now. Won't you tell me to stay?" (508–9)

To this simple romantic story, Wright adds a fictionalized account of the inner workings of finance capitalism, of locals fighting the big eastern money machine. In the novel, the Imperial Valley is called King's Basin and in order to realize its agricultural potential, the local banker Jefferson Worth must invite a group of eastern capitalists to form the King's Basin Land and Irrigation Company. Like the CDC of real history, the King's Basin Company becomes a tangle of moneyed interests and personality disputes. The East

Coast investors are portrayed as capitalists without conscience, involved in the irrigation project only for its projected returns on their investment. They quickly build shabby company towns and even shabbier irrigation dams and intakes.

After coming to a spiritual epiphany in the desert one night, Jefferson Worth determines to use capital for the good of the local people and plots secretly to form his own irrigation company. Venturing every cent he has, the crafty local capitalist and native son Abe Lee draw up alternate irrigation plans. These regional plans more accurately reflect the valley's geography, taking advantage of natural dry channels and changes in the desert's elevation to create cheap and safe passages for the irrigation flow. Worth's guerrilla irrigation project is centered in a new southern town site called Barba, near the place where the orphaned girl was discovered fifteen years earlier.

The last half of the novel focuses on the sparring between Jefferson Worth and the eastern capitalists' leader, James Greenfield. To Greenfield, the local people are nothing more than pawns. He thinks nothings of risking their lives and land. Instead of focusing on the threat of Colorado River flooding, Greenfield is obsessed with bankrupting Worth and taking over the entire valley. By putting the squeeze on western banks, Greenfield makes it impossible for Worth to draw out the money he needs to pay the Mexican and Cocopa Indian laborers who have set out his irrigation ditches, electrical plant, town sites, and rail lines.

When the angry workers strike, forming an ominous racial mob, rivals Abe Lee and Willard Holmes are thrown together in an heroic horseback dash from the coast to the valley bringing money that Worth has coaxed out of George Cartwright, an old-style capitalist much in the mold of real-life valley booster, George Chaffey. Braving an ambush by Mexican bandits, the two manage to get the funds to the valley before the labor riot erupts—just in time for the Colorado to burst its banks, drive into the King Basin, and wash away the eastern water project.

As the floodwaters recede, it becomes apparent that Jefferson Worth's intakes and ditches have held, and he and the local people stand triumphant. They have gained water for the southern fields, with the added bonus that the flow through his newly constructed hydroelectric plant is so ample that it is possible to light the local city at night.

The novel's twin plots—one charting the "rise" of a water project that is threatened by greed and redeemed by altruism, the other, tracing a young woman's search for a love that will unite all the novel's disparate forces—work together to "understand" the Imperial Valley in a new way.

The plots are woven together with a pair of time-honored themes in Anglo American myth. The first is that of individualistic adventurers chosen by God to blaze trails of progress through a biblical "wilderness." In the second, the land to be conscripted for the service of empire, nation, or capitalism is figured as a woman. This blend of mythic history and romance gives the novel its powerful moral vision, in which marriage and family replace contracts and corporations as the fundamental units of social progress.

Throughout the novel, Wright insists that both the land and its reclamation are ultimately the work of a Christian God. He overlays a Christian patina on stock regionalist depictions of desert aesthetics, claiming that the natives call the Salton Basin *La Palma de la Mano de Dios* and that the valley retains the aura of God's hand in its reclamation. Like other American stories of mastering the new world, Wright's tale endorses an Edenic social structure rooted in Protestantism and capitalism. His world is inhabited by a racially divided working class, people of "limited means" who depend for their survival on engineers, bankers, and benevolent patriarchs. The people are led, in other words, by Anglo-Saxon visionaries. Wright further Christianizes the reclamation project by casting Barbara as a latter-day Moses, a foundling of unknown heritage discovered in the wilderness and destined to lead a people to greatness. Her adoptive father, in turn, receives his special calling after wandering lost and alone in the desert.

It is also through the desert's agency that Jefferson worth experiences his epiphany. Halfway through the novel he returns to the wash where he first discovered Barbara years earlier. As he ponders their strange fate, a coyote spooks his horse, leaving him stranded in the arid waste. Night falls, and Worth receives a vision:

> And there, alone—held close in The Hollow of God's Hand as the long hours of the night passed—the spirit of the man's Puritan fathers stirred within him. In the silent, naked heart of the desert that, knowing no hand but the hand of its Creator, seemed to hold in its hushed mysteriousness the ages of a past eternity, he felt his life to be but a little thing. Besides the awful forces that made themselves felt in the spirit of Barbara's Desert, the might of Capital became small and trivial. Sensing the dreadful power that had wrought to make that land, he shrank within himself—he was afraid. He marveled that he had dared dream of forcing La Palma de la Mano de Dios to contribute to his gains. And so it was given to him at last why Barbara instinctively shrank from him in fear. (162)

Described as gray and expressionless, with a bottom-line mentality, Jefferson Worth seems an unlikely vehicle for the Almighty's work. But this desert vision washes him clean of rapacious capitalism.

In its place arises a selflessness that reaches back to the spirit of the Puritans, the most sacred of Anglo-Saxon mythic ancestors. In Jefferson Worth the desert imagery of the Old and New Testaments and the American "pilgrim" imagery of a people set in a wilderness to do God's work, come together in a modern, entrepreneurial capitalist form. In 1911, many Americans felt a nagging anxiety that they were losing their grip on the course of American history. They were thus reassured by a Pilgrim myth in which heroic Protestants found a wilderness nation to further the progress of Western European culture. In response, Harold Bell Wright makes race a central issue in his story of the Imperial Valley's reclamation, drawing heavily on the masculine adventure tradition.

Barbara softens the harsh outlines of this tradition and the reality behind it. When the men find her, her cry for water echoes that of the land Rockwood heard back in the 1890s. But unlike the real-world story of sordid business deals, engineering blunders, and federal obstacles, *The Winning of Barbara Worth* achieves the desert's reclamation by "winning" the hand of the virginal girl and by reconciling her to her adoptive father.

Each of the men who try to save Barbara are symbolic representatives of the forces Wright saw at work in the Imperial Valley reclamation project. Abe Lee, whose name offers an idealistic resolution of the Civil War's sectional rivalries, acts "like one of Cooper's Leather-Stocking heroes" (406). He thus functions like a nineteenth-century frontiersman in early novels of the American West, as a cultural go-between, balancing American Indian knowledge of nature with Anglo-Saxon hard work and values. Lincolnesque, like Harold Bell Wright himself, Abe Lee "can out-walk, out-work, out-last and out-guess any man. . . . He has the instinct of a wild animal for finding his way and the coldest nerve" ever seen (81). He is, however, a bastard, and so cannot claim the kind of racial purity necessary to the Anglo-Saxon myths of the West. He can only be a sidekick to the novel's real culture heroes, Jefferson Worth and Willard Holmes.

Willard Holmes is meant to win Barbara's hand and to engineer the reclamation of the desert by means of Jefferson Worth's capital. He is of pure Anglo-Saxon stock and is remade by his desert experience. Late in the novel we learn that his "conception and understanding of his work as an engineer had changed materially in the years since those first days with Barbara in Rubio City. It may have been that in his long, lonely rides . . . something of the spirits of the slow, silent ages . . . had touched his spirit" (364).

Even Holmes cannot claim the title of true hero in the story, however. That role is reserved for Jefferson Worth, who is also carved out of American adventure mythology. His name connotes the Jeffersonian yeoman farmer ideal of the West, but his antecedents are the Massachusetts Puritans. He also has a "super-human instinct for Good Business," and to the other characters in the novel becomes "the visible representative of that invisible power that willed their going forth. He was Capital—Money—Business incarnate" (144).

Neither adventurer nor engineer, he is a new creation in the canon of American adventure lore and reflects a larger shift going on in American culture from entrepreneurial to managerial capitalism. As cultural historian Jackson Lears describes it, turn-of-the-century America was becoming increasingly bureaucratized. In the "workplace, school, and home, managerial and professional elites were appropriating authority and decision making power from ordinary citizens" (Lears 303). Jefferson Worth is an antidote to this trend. He is a hands-on, single, and solitary entrepreneur, risking his own capital in difficult projects with the hope of big returns.

But he does it all in the name of something Wright calls "Good Business," capitalism from the heart, capitalism for the good of humanity. His heroic attitudes are racial and inherited, and thus part of a larger cosmopolitan dream in which the white race would be reinvigorated by the challenges of places like the Imperial Valley. Good business was a new kind of heroism. To men like Jefferson Worth, "business . . . was his profession, but it was even more than a profession; it was the expression of his genius. Still more it was, through him, the expression of the age in which he lived, the expression of the master passion that in all ages had wrought in the making of the race" (158).

Wright's story about the Imperial Valley caught the imagination of readers in the first half of the twentieth century precisely because it so artfully wielded these mythic and racial ideals in the service of a story that Sam Goldwyn called "drama itself." When the narrator finally observes that "Barbara and her Desert had won against the Company through Willard Holmes" (376), we realize that land and race have come together seamlessly to resolve the dilemma faced by the reclamationists: how to transform a corporate expansionist scheme into a pioneering, mythic, and Christian enterprise. As the "true representative of a true womanhood that holds in itself the future of the race," Barbara's story is a reflection of the reclamation story. She waits for her hero "even as the desert held in its earth womb life for the strong one whom the slow years fitted to realize it" (290).

Although at heart a cosmopolitan dream, *The Winning of Barbara Worth* also appealed to locals. When the novel was published, Wright became an instant valley celebrity. He gave speeches, dispensed wisdom, opened the opera house, posed for portraits. In 1915, through the financial efforts of W. F. Holt, the Barbara Worth Hotel opened in El Centro. It was both an oasis for tourists and travelers and a monument to Wright's mythic version of the valley's reclamation. The lobby was inscribed with a quotation from the book: "The desert waited, silent, hot and fierce in its desolation, holding its treasures against the coming of the strong ones." Eleven life-size murals graced the walls, each depicting a scene from Wright's story. Painted by Chicago artists Edward Vysikel and Luvena Buchanan, the murals bore titles like "Desolation," "Primitive Life," "Capital Enlisted," and "Labor" (see figure 7).

The centerpiece was a huge mural on the north wall entitled "The Conquest of the Desert." Using real valley pioneers as models, the artists sketched out the contours of the reclamation myth. Otis Tout, a valley historian, recalls seeing the original for the first time:

> The west edge of the picture depicts the desert, real, tawny and severe. Signal Mountain and the purple skyline of the San Jacintos form the background. In the center stands a life size figure lifting an irrigation gate and turning the water upon the barren land. This figure while being symbolic was posed by Charles N. Perry, who was on the spot when this historical event actually took place, even if he did not actually lift the gate. To the left, stand Willard Holmes and Barbara Worth as they stood at the close of the story. Into the scene from the extreme right comes an interesting group. A pioneer, his wife and child, a figure representing Agriculture holding by the hand a figure representing the trades followed closely by a figure representing the Industries. Trade is leading Culture, a beautiful young woman. In the corner stands the Golden Page, representing on a golden tray the Rewards of Industry. (199)

The artwork and the novel served as backdrops for the lives of cosmopolitans like Edward Ayer and his wife. Tourists like them, passing through the region, were immersed in the progressive sweep of Wright's vision, which could explain the western lands they would later view from their railcar windows.

FIGURE 7. Leo Hetzel, *Lobby, Barbara Worth Hotel.*
Imperial County Historical Society.

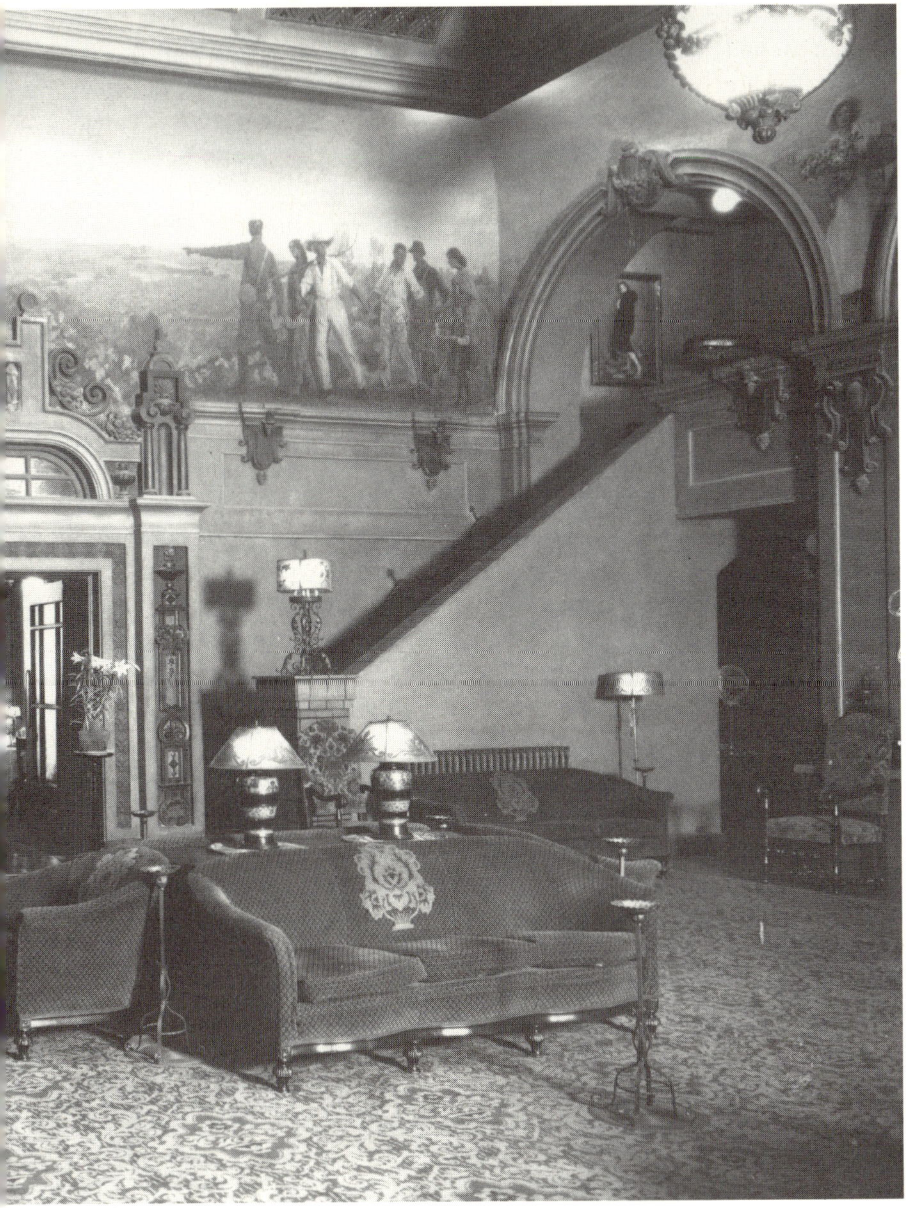

But the hotel was more than that. It was also a shrine to people who lived in the valley, and they took its lessons to heart. Up on the wall, if you looked closely at "Culture," you could just make out Miss Sawyer, a schoolteacher from Meloland. It was a fine thing, this blending of the local and the cosmopolitan, so fine a thing that Otis Tout felt sure the painting would "stand for the ages."

It did not. The Barbara Worth Hotel, mythic monument to water, was engulfed in flames in 1962 and burned to the ground. Just before he left the valley for good in 1916, Wright himself torched the Tecolote Rancho hut where he had written the novel. In the 1960s local patrons of the arts tried to preserve what was left of Wright's house as a monument to valley literature, but they could rouse little interest in the project.

One of those who tried to celebrate Wright's role in valley storytelling was my aunt, Yvonne Smith, who lived in the valley for fifty years and was once county chairman of the Republican Party. She was a great collector of Americana. One never knew if the box in the mail from her would contain a paperweight from the Nixon Library, a piece of the White House floating in an acrylic block suitable for display, or a ceramic bust of an American eagle. In the fall of 2001, the package I got contained a brick. She had heard I was writing a book about the desert, her note said, and this was an original piece of Harold Bell Wright's Tecolote Rancho. Somehow, she reasoned, that brick would bring me closer to the Imperial Valley's great brush with literary history, closer to Wright's spirit and the spirit of place that his novel still embodies for long-time residents like herself. Even at the beginning of the twenty-first century, for locals like my aunt, Wright's vision held true. "Capital—Money—Business," to be sure, but also the sacred place and beauty that only the favored few, the connoisseurs could see—as Otis Tout described it, "real, tawny, severe."

My aunt's brick—my brick—sits on my office bookshelf staring at me as I write this, an inscrutable reminder of the nature of place and storytelling. Undeniably real, as material as anything can be, it beckons from that shelf with an allure that perfectly epitomizes the stubborn realities that ground myths of place such as those Harold Bell Wright spun about California's "inland empire."

4 American Exodus

| In the spring of 1937, twenty years after Harold Bell Wright left the region he had made famous, the noted documentary photographer Dorothea Lange began working in the Imperial Valley. She wrote to a government official in Washington about her experiences in the place: "Down here if they don't like you they shoot at you and give you the works. Beat you up and throw you into a ditch at the county line." Two years later Charles Todd put it more polemically in an article written for *Common Sense*: "The forces of stupidity and wrath [have] made the Valley a sink-hole of farm labor exploitation since the days of the first irrigating ditch" (7). Residents of the valley told a different story. One local preacher described outsiders like Lange as people "who would tear the white and blue out of Old Glory and leave you a red flag" (quoted in Andres 283). He exhorted his followers to applaud the officers who had beat up an ACLU representative, calling them "two-fisted, and hard-hitting" representatives of "100% Americanism" (283). Another resident bragged, "We have an excellent formula for getting rid of cockroaches, grasshoppers, and CIO agitators" (248).

In the 1930s, most of the stories about the Imperial Valley were polarized like this—black or white, red-baiting or antifascist. The thousands of hungry migrant farmers who had come to valley from faraway places like Arkansas, Oklahoma, and Guanajuato were caught somewhere in between.

The reason for the violent divergence in 1930s stories about the valley was in many ways simple and familiar. Once gain, the Imperial Valley was being touted, in the words of sociologist Paul Schuster Taylor, as "the last west." This "last west" was perhaps the toughest of all. *American Exodus*, the book Taylor co-wrote with Dorothea Lange in 1940, explains why:

> For three centuries an ever-receding western frontier has drawn white men like a magnet. This tradition still draws distressed, dislodged, determined Americans to our last West, hard against the waters of the Pacific. But settlement and mechanization have transformed our frontier. The land is already occupied, and men work upon it with machines as in factories, or at hand labor in gangs as in industry. Highways are part of the process of mechanization. Over their hard surfaces the harvested crops move in great truckloads to market, and a labor reserve rolls in from as far east as the Mississippi to mill ceaselessly back and forth through the valleys of California following the crops. This opportunity to obtain intermittent employment in a disorganized labor market—no experience required—is our new frontier, our new West. (107)

American Exodus is a picture book with a conscience. It grew out of Paul Taylor's sociological research on the dust bowl and Dorothea Lange's documentary photographs of the plight of migrant workers, many of them taken in the Imperial Valley. *American Exodus* reflects an era in American storytelling pervaded by "national self-scrutiny," to use the words of Alfred Kazin. "Upon a tripod of photographs, captions, and text," Taylor and Lange invoke a new kind of morality tale, melding regionalist description with sociological method (Lange and Taylor 6).

Once again, the Imperial Valley was at the center of this new examination of the meaning of the American western landscape, but this time the focus was on labor and the narrative point of view was scientific. Obviously, this represented a real turnaround from the reclamationist storytelling project. To Harold Bell Wright, labor was a necessary but invisible element in Jefferson Worth's great engineering triumphs. When labor does appear in *The Winning of Barbara Worth* it is as a menacing force, dark at the edges and simmering with violence. It is "a stirring, restless mass of men, shadowy and indistinct." What made the valley great was Worth's perseverance, not the anonymous scrabbling of lower-class workers.

Wright's romantic gilding aside, however, agricultural labor in the Golden State was and always had been quite different from that in the rest of America. When the Depression caused the national spotlight to shine on the industrial and technological enterprise that was farming in the Imperial Valley, this reality began to cut through the reclamationist myths.

California agriculture epitomized modernity in all of its glory and gloom. Labor historian Cletus E. Daniel has pointed out that "the large-scale agriculture of California did not represent a departure from the dominant family-farming tradition in America for the simple reason that California was never part of that tradition" (18). In California, "the nation was afforded its first look at agriculture in truly modern dress" (39).

From the very beginning in the Imperial Valley, cutting-edge irrigation technologies and finance capitalism had turned farming into a fundamentally industrial enterprise. With its year-round growing season and staggering productivity, the valley required manual laborers in numbers that dwarfed the needs of the nineteenth-century family farm. Meanwhile, the incredible variety of crops and increasingly mechanized production meant that these large gangs of workers were needed only during peak harvest weeks. The rest of the time, they were discouraged from making the valley their home. This unusual labor demand—large numbers of workers employed for short, concentrated effort only during certain times of the year—became the unlikely source of much of the valley "literature" written in the twenties and thirties. During these boom years, Imperial Valley growers developed an elaborate public relations system to attract workers to the area for harvests. In addition to cutting a deal with the Southern Pacific railroad, which offered "colonist" rates for workers willing to travel west, growers put together the California Promotion Committee, a group that published tantalizing leaflets and stereopticon shows to lure farmers and laborers to the region. *The Winning of Barbara Worth* was in a sense part of this promotional period of Imperial Valley agriculture. By the 1920s, a powerful landowning elite combined with a surplus work force to create an agricultural system that "could not perpetuate itself without a captive peasantry" (Daniel 61).

As the nation sank into economic depression, the Imperial Valley's unique situation was thrown into high relief. As drought laid waste to America's traditional farms, the Imperial Valley became something of an Eden in the national imagination. One of Lange's dust-bowl interviewees explained its mystique, "I heerd tell of this here irrigation, plenty of water and plenty to eat" (135). *American Exodus* makes it clear, however, that the water and food were the prerogative of a select few.

Will Rogers made outright fun of the Imperial Valley's labor and investment campaigns, calling the valley "a freak of nature" that "some old preacher had named." The valley's potent blend of evangelism and development apotheosized in *The Winning of Barbara Worth* inspired Rogers's diatribe about a promotional tour he was given there. "There is a good big lake down there and it's all salt," Rogers reported,

> But the real estate men and the Chamber of Commerce passed a resolution and either it or them had to get out. Well the Lord saw that while he might be able to handle nature, He couldn't do anything with California Real estate men. It was a new form of pestilence that he had never encountered before. So he just washed his hands of the whole thing, picked up his ocean and took it down into Mexico, where they appreciated God's original handiwork, and the Preachers were not selling Real Estate. (92)

Rogers had good fun spinning counternarratives to the valley's marketing myths, claiming that "the town of Calipatria was named by taking a part of two famous historical names. The Cal, comes from Calvin Coolidge—first name of Calvin, and the Patria, comes from the last part of CleoPatria, a woman of doubtful reputation, who I am sorry to see Mr. Coolidge get mixed up with" (93).

Imperial Valley residents retaliated with new, harder-edged stories of their own. In these, outsiders became "agitators" and "terrorists" who were looking to leave only a "red flag" in their wake. During the thirties, valley residents voiced their fears in local papers. They articulated those suspicions in the now-established mythic conception of the valley depicted on the walls of the Barbara Worth Hotel. As labor organizers flooded into the valley, some spouting Communist Party rhetoric, the sense that this pastoral utopia was coming under siege from new and frightening forces produced an increasingly shrill anticommunist polemic. "It is a sorry situation," one local wrote, "if a group of outsiders is permitted to come in at this time to interrupt tranquility" (Andres 296). The valley was beginning to look, another grower said, like "some country other than America" (307).

The struggle between local and "outside" cosmopolitan visions of what the valley meant in terms of the larger picture of America came to a head in 1934, the worst year of labor strife in valley history. Historian Benny Andres records that "from January 1933 to the summer of 1939, there were 180 strikes in thirty-four of [California's] fifty-eight counties" (288). A full one-third of the agricultural labor force in the state was on strike during these years. The Imperial Valley, with its uniquely modern farm labor requirements, became the epicenter of the national debate over agricultural workers rights, particularly those of migrant Americans uprooted by the dust bowl. "Federal" rights, those protections granted by fiat from Washington, often ran counter to what local elites felt was in their region's best interest.

During this period, labor and growers engaged in a brutal war in which many workers were killed and countless others beaten up and sent packing. But there was also a war of words, of stories about the meaning of the Imperial Valley. Literary regionalism played an important role in the valley's reappearance on the national stage in the thirties, and it would shape the dialogue between locals and outsiders for the next ten years. The combined vision of imported labor activists and Washington lawmakers impacted the Imperial Valley in the 1930s with surprising results that transcended the historical moment that created them. Dorothea Lange went to the valley to take pictures for the government, but the work she produced there has outlasted both the labor struggle it chronicled and the aesthetic of documentary photography that it founded.

Lange's career began when she came out west in 1918, after having apprenticed in portrait photography with Arnold Genthe in New York. Genthe had himself been a major force in early western American photography; he is now most often remembered for his candid shots of San Francisco's Chinatown. By the time Lange worked for him, however, Genthe's interests had changed. What Lange learned from him was a savvy sense of how to earn money in portrait photography by making the client look as attractive as possible. Genthe had taken the realism of his early work and used it to transform the studio head shot. His portraits are remarkable for their vibrancy and ability to capture a sitter's charisma. He also tutored Lange in the judicious use of retouching and other darkroom techniques that would make prints seem more "real."

When Lange arrived in San Francisco in 1918, she set up shop as a portrait photographer and was soon making a good living. Her social circle encompassed many of the most innovative western artists of the day. At the age of twenty-four she met and married the acclaimed western artist and illustrator Maynard Dixon. For fifteen years she lived with Dixon and shared in his exploration of the Southwest, traveling to Navajo country in 1923 and to Taos in 1930. During these years, her portrait photography took a back seat to Dixon's painting, but she learned a great deal from him about art and the West.

In a sense, Maynard Dixon was the man John Van Dyke had wanted to be. When Dixon sought inspiration, he retreated to the desert. What he found there was

> a reality that appears unreal, challenging the imagination.... You cannot argue with silence. It returns your questions to you, to your own inner silence which becomes aware—a mystical something that is neither reason nor intelligence nor intuition. (Dixon 41)

Dixon was most famous in his day for his illustrations in *Sunset* magazine and the *Overland Monthly*, and for his genre paintings of cowboys and Indians. Today, however, his "serious" easel paintings from the thirties, with their distinctive use of color and application, are some of the most sought-after images of western light and deserts.

During one excursion to New Mexico with Dixon, Lange began to experiment with photography out of doors, on the fly, stopping the car for a moment to get a shot. It was far cry from the carefully controlled studio techniques she had perfected in her portrait business, but it seems to have appealed to her, giving her both a sense of freedom and of immersion in nature. On a trip to the California backcountry in 1929, on a mountain during a thunderstorm, she had a vision that would change her photography forever: "It came to me what I had to do was to take pictures of people, only people, all kinds of people. People who paid me and people who didn't" (Meltzer 63).

On May Day 1933 that vision gained a mission. In the street protests of San Francisco's working men and women, Lange saw for the first time visceral proof of "the discrepancy between what she was working on in the frames, and what was going on in the street" (Meltzer 70). Within a year, Lange left Maynard Dixon to follow her calling to employ documentary photography in the service of the people. In her new liberal social circle, she met Paul Shuster Taylor, a native of Iowa who had returned from combat in World War I to pursue an academic career in sociology at the University of California. Taylor was at the forefront of a group of activist sociologists that the Roosevelt administration was consulting for advice about how best to deal with the Depression. One of Taylor's most important contributions was his incorporation of documentary photography into his statistical surveys of the exploitation of migrant labor and other social ills. He began using a camera to document case studies in the 1920s, and by the 1930s had decided that photography needed to be a regular and institutional part of sociology.

Taylor and Lange met on a 1934 expedition he had helped to arrange with Immogen Cunningham, Preston Holder, and Mary Jeanette Edwards. The group traveled to photograph a federal sawmill cooperative near the foothill community of Oroville, California. From that time forward, Lange and Taylor formed a partnership in life, art, and activism. The following year, they took a working honeymoon to the Imperial Valley.

In a sense, Dorothea Lange came of age as a photographer in the Imperial Valley. The Lower Colorado Desert would become a recurring touchstone in her photographic studies of the "human erosion" of America in the thirties. The valley served as the backdrop for Lange's birth as a serious artist and became the regional "place" in which she found herself and her role in American art. In the process, she became the valley's most important storyteller of the period, articulating a vision of the reclaimed desert that focused on its human costs. Her portraits of Imperial Valley migrant laborers celebrate their humanity but also reveal a fascination with the technology that made the valley such an anomaly during the drought years. All told, Lange visited and photographed the valley four times during the period March 1935 through the spring of 1939.

Dorothea Lange cut a pretty cosmopolitan figure in the Imperial Valley in 1935 with her men's trousers and boots and her signature beret. Despite her flamboyance, Lange really managed to connect with the people she photographed in the valley. She would stride right up and engage them in conversation, or kneel down with them in the alkaline dirt, Rollex on her left shoulder, a palm-sized notebook balanced in her right hand, as she recorded word snapshots of conversations she had with her subjects: "Mexican father born in old country—came here—Mar. 1924—Mother, came from Iowa—1920" (Brown 21). Part of Lange's storytelling goal was to make these "outsiders" human and real to the readers of the magazines in which her photographs appeared. They are regular Americans, just like you, her pictures seem to say.

During most of her excursions to the Imperial Valley, Lange worked under the auspices of the Farm Security Administration (FSA) as a "photographer-investigator." The FSA was dedicated to the "rehabilitation of poor people" in rural America. Part of the agency's mandate was to document the history of the rural poor, as well as any inroads the government might be making into improving their situation. Roy Stryker was the head of the FSA's Historical Section. A graduate in economics from Columbia University, Stryker believed that photography could aid the FSA effort by allowing its audience to experience "not only what a place or thing looks like, but . . . also what it would feel like to be an actual witness to the scene"

(Bezner 10). Stryker was, by all accounts, a stern taskmaster and sometimes an ideologue, but he got his photographers to produce some of the best work of their careers.

In many ways, the FSA photographs of the Imperial Valley and other rural places are the work of a cosmopolitan imagination. The agency was centered in Washington, where the negatives were turned into prints and distributed to national media outlets at a rate of several thousand per month. The FSA collection of photographs from the thirties tends to reflect one seamless "rural" America—threadbare and drought struck—in which various regions meld together into a generalized "outside." The FSA photographs are peopled by laboring *types*—"ditch dwellers, bindle stiffs, . . . pea pickers." Paul Taylor and Dorothea Lange worried about this tendency on the part of the FSA to homogenize regional difference. When they produced their own work about the dust bowl, they cautioned readers, "We show you what is happening in selected regions of limited area. Something is lost by this method, for it fails to show fully the wide extent and the many variations of rural changes which we describe. But we believe that the gain in sharpness of focus reveals better the nature of the changes themselves" (6).

Dorothea Lange's efforts to present a "sharp focus" story about the Imperial Valley was at odds with both local myths and FSA cosmopolitan activism precisely because it accentuated those regional differences that made the Imperial Valley an exceptional locale in 1930s America. Lange's photographs bring together the Imperial Valley's unique combination of modern industrial agriculture, "elemental" light, and human misery in ways that far exceed most critics' response to their "documentary" qualities. In contrast to Harold Bell Wright, who focused on the "grand forces" at work in the valley's history, Lange was interested in the individual. Her distinctive approach to achieving a clear-eyed image of the region was, surprisingly, through individual portraiture. She tied her portraits to interviews with the men and women who sat to have their pictures taken alongside barrow pits and fields, between shifts and during water breaks.

The valley's arid desert background provided Lange with unique opportunities for uncovering the "feeling" of the rural laborers who were her subjects. It is illuminating to compare two portraits that were published at about the same time. *Migrant Mother*, Lange's most famous portrait, was taken in Nipomo, in central California (see figure 8). Critics have discussed at length the compositional power of the children clustered about their mother, her careworn and distracted gaze. There is also, however, the setting, which is a tent—quite literally, canvas. Its effect is to render this image as an aesthetic object, even as it claims sociological "reality."

The facing page portrait is quite different (see figure 9). Taken in the Imperial Valley, it is captioned *Old Mexican Laborer*, and the face and posture of its subject are etched against a vast emptiness. The expressionless gray sky of the valley offers barely a hint of horizon over the subject's left shoulder. His distracted gaze is transported beyond careworn by this haunted, suspending quality of the background. With the attenuated horizon and no middle ground, the man's head and shoulders are elongated in a manner reminiscent of El Greco. Where the Nipomo mother is a modern Virgin Mary, the Mexican man is figure from the Old Testament. In a landscape without traditional aesthetic value—bleak, barren, and empty—he becomes Job or a wandering Israelite.

Because the valley's landscape denied Lange even the bare aesthetic drapery she had found in the migrant camps of central California, it forced her to focus with absolute intensity on the human form. In two other portraits of Imperial Valley workers, Lange manages to shift the landscape from desolate to sublime. The subjects' humanity emerges even more strongly from the background of the valley's immense distances. In the first, a young woman field worker has pushed back her hat to reveal an intriguing face and enigmatic, Mona Lisa smile (figure 10).

In the second, two men, otherwise alone in the universe, strike postures of camaraderie and conversation that belie the emptiness of the space around them (figure 11). The guitar hanging from one man's shoulder invokes music as the sound of human emotion that triumphs over the desert's silence.

Imperial Valley landscapes also gave Lange a chance to represent some of the ineluctable abstract forces that lay behind the Depression and the dust bowl. Irrigated farming, the cutting edge of modern agriculture, underscored the inadequacies of the nineteenth-century approaches to crop production still used in Oklahoma, Arkansas, and Texas. In her notebook, Lange reminded herself to "emphasize reclaimed desert." It was a "desert method" she saw, and she set out to photograph specifically "desert agriculture."

Many of Lange's pictures of Imperial Valley farms stress the immensity of the modern industrial farming complex. In these images, Lange employs far-distant vanishing points to affect a sort of infinite regress of agricultural abundance (figure 12). That abundance is given an eerie quality in pictures that Lange notes were taken at "high noon," a time when no shadows are cast and thus no immediate perspective can be achieved.

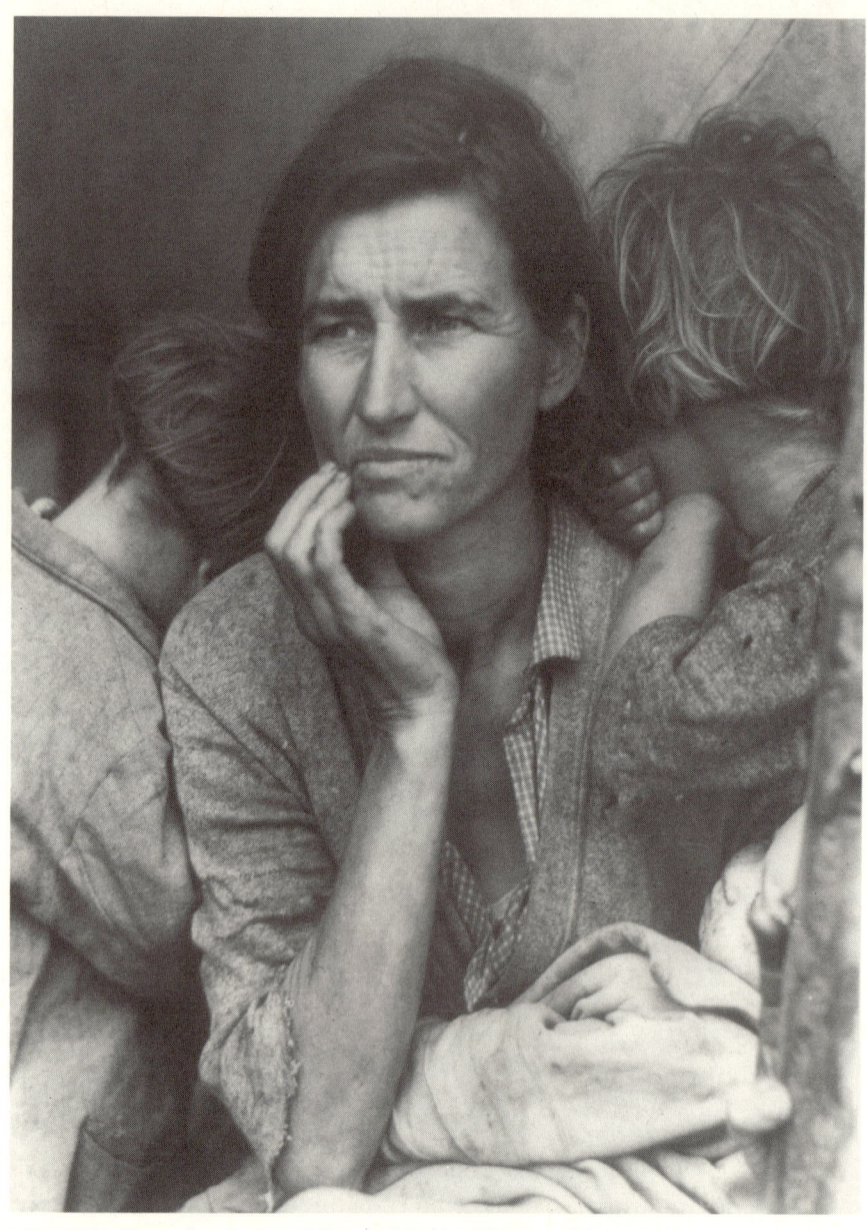

FIGURE 8. Dorothea Lange, *Migrant Mother*. Library of Congress, Prints & Photographs Division, FSA-OWI Collection, [LC-DIG-fsa-8b29516 DLC].

FIGURE 9. Dorothea Lange, *Old Mexican Laborer Saying, "I Have Worked All My Life and All I Have Now Is My Broken Body."* Library of Congress, Prints & Photographs Division, FSA-OWI Collection, [LC-USF34-001618-C].

FIGURE 10. Dorothea Lange, *Mexican Girl Who Picks Peas for the Eastern Market*. Library of Congress, Prints & Photographs Division, FSA-OWI Collection, [LC-USF34-019171-E].

FIGURE 11. Dorothea Lange, *One of the Roads Leading into Calipatria, Imperial County, California*. Library of Congress, Prints & Photographs Division, FSA-OWI Collection, [LC-USF34-019046-E].

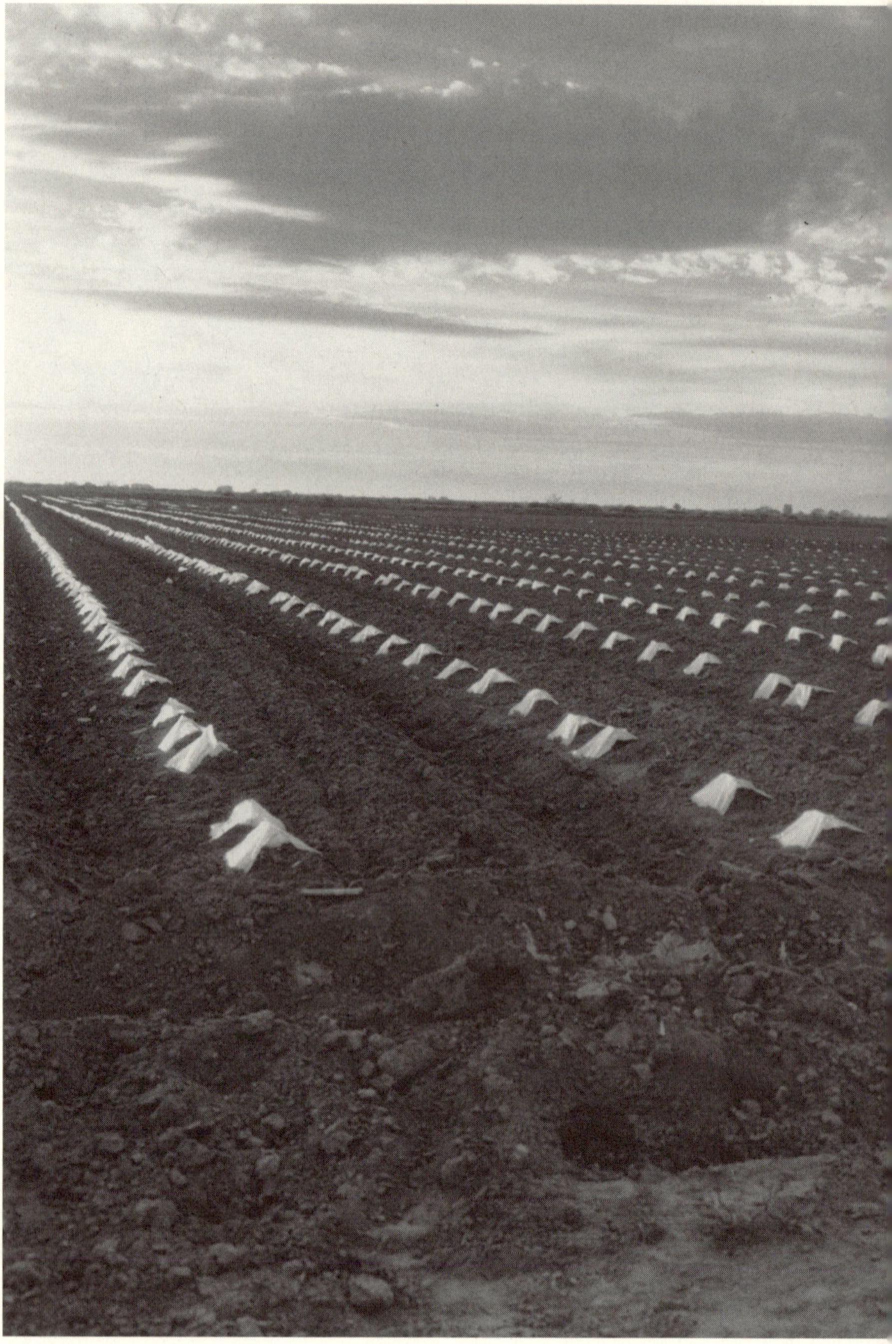

FIGURE 12. Dorothea Lange, *Capped Cantaloupe. Imperial Valley, California.* Library of Congress, Prints & Photographs Division, FSA-OWI Collection, [LC-USF34-016134-C].

To further highlight the modernity of the valley's agriculture, Lange trained her lens on the new technologies being employed there. In one image of the valley's many canals (figure 13), Lange anchors the background palms that suggest a desert oasis to the strong horizontal foreground line of the irrigation head gate. Here, the vanishing point works to instill a narrative sense of progress in the scene. In another photograph of the valley's irrigation technology (figure 14), Lange counterpoises the immense weight and linearity of a steam dredge shovel against the irregular landscape of the valley's unreclaimed, mountain margins. The machine and cement culvert are rich, deep blacks and grays, making the desert middle landscape and the extremely elongated sky seem washed out by comparison. As in the image of the irrigation head gate, this picture provides some progressive narrative potential in its compositional scheme, with the dredge's great arm reaching skyward toward a brighter future.

When Lange grafted her Imperial Valley "desert agriculture" images onto her desert portrait style, she forged a new kind of storytelling. The result was a tale that was immediate, visceral, and among the most "on the ground" of any told during the Depression. Her collection of photos of Imperial Valley laborers enunciates a new story about the region, one that sets human beings against the vast reclaimed desert then finds that they are dwarfed by the very technology they have engaged to "save the desert from itself." In such images, Lange carefully balances scenes of an alienated labor force with landscape pastoral in such a way as to offer a complex analysis of the human/labor/landscape relation.

One such image (figure 15) situates the viewer deep in a furrow, below even the stooped laborers. Already immersed in earth and vegetation, the viewer's earthbound point of view is reinforced by an exposure level that warms the scene, thus increasing the feeling of envelopment. Although "documentary," the picture's political power derives from something quite different than realism or truth. It is an image worthy of Buñuel or Orozco.

Another photograph Lange took of valley workers is similarly rooted in the earth (figure 16). This time the valley's landscape is clodded earth, making the laborers' tasks appear Herculean. In this picture, the workers' hats make an important compositional and editorial point. They both protect them from the valley's unforgiving sun and mask their individuality, underscoring the dehumanizing effect of the "desert method" of agriculture.

In their foreword to *American Exodus*, Lange and Taylor spelled out the role of such photographic images in their work. "Neither a book of photographs, nor an illustrated book" (5), *American Exodus* was intended to be a modern, rational blending of art and science. "We adhere to the standards of documentary photography as we have conceived them," she and Taylor explain, adding that "quotations which accompany photographs report what the persons photographed said, not what we think might be their unspoken thoughts" (6).

Dorothea Lange's Imperial Valley photographs also represent an attempt to alter the nature of narrative in the American West. In published interviews and private notes, Lange insisted that photographs must be "read." She believed that photographic prints represented a "sort of short hand," that a story emerged from the juxtaposition of image and caption. Her pictures told their tales "by suggestions, to one who is willing to *read* [them], rather than look at them." Lange didn't care for "the kind of written material that tells a person what to look for" in a photograph. Words should be limited, she felt, to providing a picture with "more background," to fortifying it "without directing the person's mind" (Brown 64).

This melding of storytelling and "scientific" documentary photograph is particularly vivid in Lange's notebook of her Imperial Valley experiences. Housed at the Oakland Museum, Lange's field notes from the Imperial Valley are comprised of catch phrases and snatches of conversation scribbled in a four-by-five inch reporter's notepad in long vertical columns. The format allows Lange's notes to unfold like lyric poetry. In the case of her observations on the dwellings of Brawley's Mexican laborers, the personal and scientific are blended to astonishing effect:

> To Brawley—
>   1 Street in Brawley
> Map of Street
>   Views of alley—am pm
>   Garbage disposal
>   Sewage
>   People
>   What they say
>   What they have
> No. of hours
> So many like this
> So many like this
>   What they earn
>   So many like this
>   So many like this
>   (Brown, vol. 2, 64)

FIGURE 13. Dorothea Lange, *Irrigation Ditch along the Road. Imperial Valley, California*. Library of Congress, Prints & Photographs Division, FSA-OWI Collection, [LC-USF34-016149-E].

FIGURE 14. Dorothea Lange, *Laguna Dam*. Library of Congress, Prints & Photographs Division, FSA-OWI Collection, [LC-USF34-016145-C].

FIGURE 15. Dorothea Lange, *Desert Agriculture. Brushed Chili Field. Replanting Chili Plants on a Japanese-owned Ranch*. Library of Congress, Prints & Photographs Division, FSA-OWI Collection, [LC-USF35-1326].

FIGURE 16. Dorothea Lange, *The Kind of Work Drought Refugees and Mexicans Do in the Imperial Valley, California*. Library of Congress, Prints & Photographs Division, FSA-OWI Collection, [LC-USF34-016114-E].

The photographs that accompany this set of notes reflect a similar balance of empathy and critical distance (figure 17). Lange took more than one hundred pictures of this Brawley neighborhood. In all of them, high-key light and sharp contrast underscore the terrible conditions in which the migrant laborers eke out their existence. The facts are there—shoddy housing, unsanitary trash disposal, dirt streets and floors—but the photographer's artistry makes them visceral for the viewer. Lange uses the presumed objectivity of photographic "science" to place the viewer firmly in the role of outsider. Through the scientific detachment of the viewfinder, her "reader" discovers the horrifying details of lives lived by contemporary Californians in the Imperial Valley. Lange's artistic achievement lay in communicating this disturbing information without editorializing or sensationalizing it.

Yet Lange consistently tempers such objectivity and scientific distance by embracing her subjects as individuals. In her notebook, we both hear and see Lange coming to consciousness of the plight of these laborers as she sits on the ground interviewing them. A particularly poignant passage in the journal unself-consciously dramatizes a misunderstanding between Lange and a native speaker of Spanish:

> Gracias Adios
>   A Dios
> Gracias A Dios.
>   (Brown 66)

What Lange came to understand in this encounter is vividly illustrated in another photograph from this visit (figure 18).

Like the Brawley pictures, this image highlights abhorrent working conditions, including the lack of running water. Again, the ironies of the modern water project are underscored by the worker's lack of access to the very thing that makes the valley great. But the photograph also moves into the mythic mode of *Migrant Mother* by exploiting the woman's posture and the compositional power of the plank walkway on which she stands. The scientific has given way to something else here, not quite religious, but akin to the humanizing movement we witness in Lange's notebook realization that what her informant meant to say was not "Thanks, good bye," but "Thanks be to God."

Lange's work from this period is as much about her role as storyteller as it is about the dust bowl and labor strife. Although Lange's pictures of the Imperial Valley seem candid—sometimes almost overexposed or even technically unsophisticated—they are carefully wrought artistic renderings of a story of place that includes the story of the role of the artist in that place. Behind the scenes, Lange fought mightily with Roy Stryker for the right to touch up and print her own negatives. Stryker was outraged, arguing that documentary photographs should remain pure, that touch-ups would "dirty" the negative and falsify the facts. Lange disagreed. She erased a distracting flaw from *Migrant Mother* to improve the photograph's aesthetic and "scientific" power. This did not alter the basic fact of the migrant laborers' destitution and despair; it enhanced her viewers' appreciation of the woman's suffering.

Lange's Imperial Valley pictures also sometimes reveal her thoughts about the role of the artist in times of national political and economic upheaval. Her photographs and notes evince a self-consciousness, an evaluation of her social role as a documentary storyteller. "A man's negatives," she once wrote "are his autobiography.... The content lies buried there. The prints are an extraction" (Brown, vol. 2, 372). This very private view of the image suggests that only the photographer can experience the negatives in their true reality. In turn, this implies that places like the Imperial Valley must be experienced directly to be truly known. Lange and Taylor were nevertheless determined to make the Imperial Valley as real as they could to readers around the country in order to spur them to action on behalf of the dust-bowl migrant families.

Lange's Imperial Valley photographs were immortalized in her and Taylor's masterpiece, *American Exodus*, a work they completed not long after their last trip to the valley in 1940. *American Exodus* is divided by geographic region, mapping the forced migration of thousands of Americans off of their farms and into cities and places far from home. Each chapter is comprised of a photo essay followed by statistical and historical analysis. Lange provided the images and interviews, and Taylor, the sociological data. As they survey "The Old South," "The Plantation Under the Machine," the "Midcontinent," and the "Plains," they take care to differentiate the geographies and economies of these regions, as well as the complex feelings of the dislocated Americans they study.

The book climaxes with the "Last West," where Lange's Imperial Valley images punctuate the finality of the laborers' arrival in California. At the end of the line, with nowhere else to go, the disillusioned workers collide with callous local growers. Lange and Taylor exploit the ironies of this place, where various and luxuriant crops—a wonder of modern irrigation technology—flourish, while the men and woman who work the fields are reduced to a life that is, as one put it, "simplicity boiled down" (135).

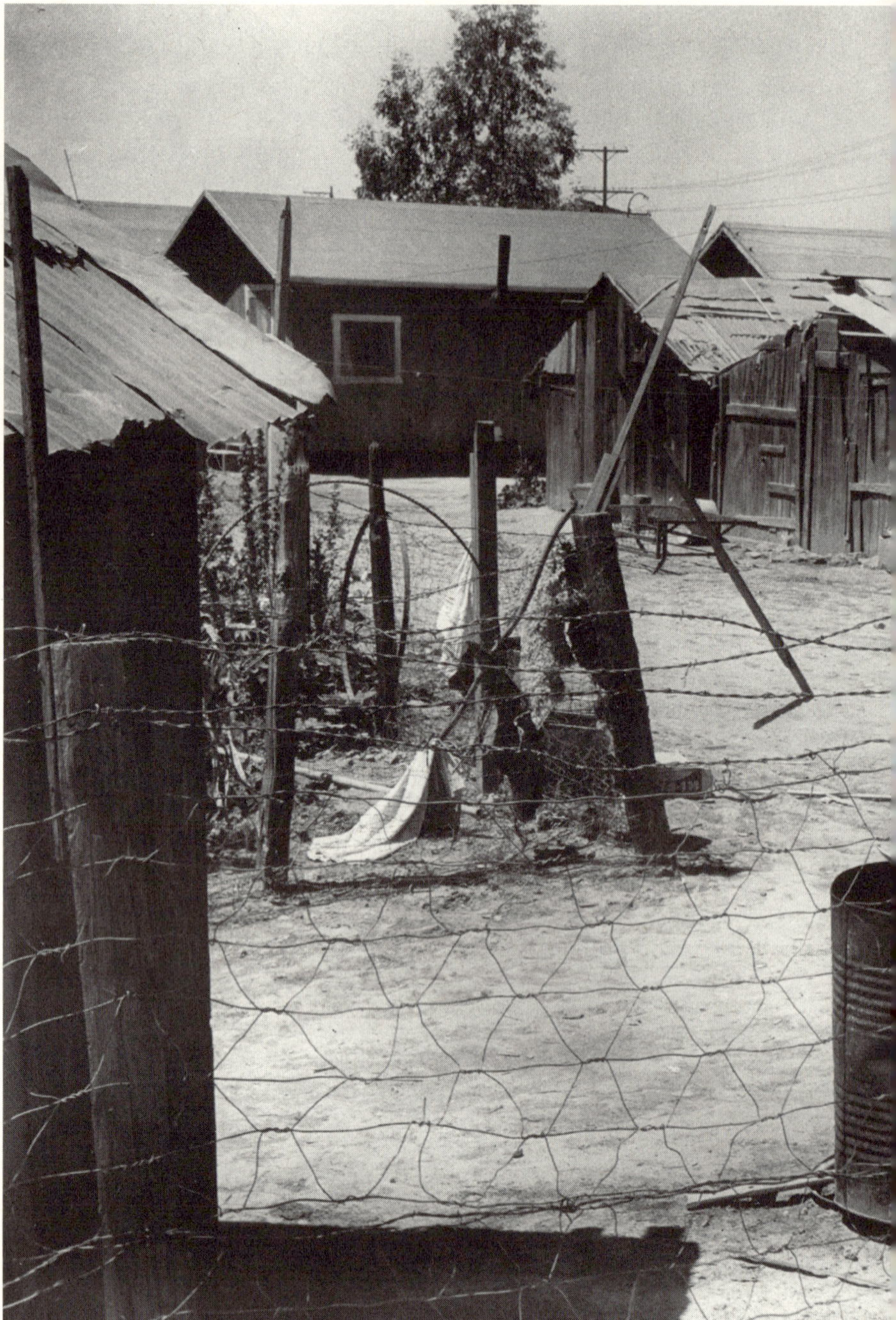

FIGURE 17.
Dorothea Lange, *Homes of Mexican Field Laborers. Brawley, Imperial Valley, California*. Library of Congress, Prints & Photographs Division, FSA-OWI Collection, [LC-USF34-002284-C].

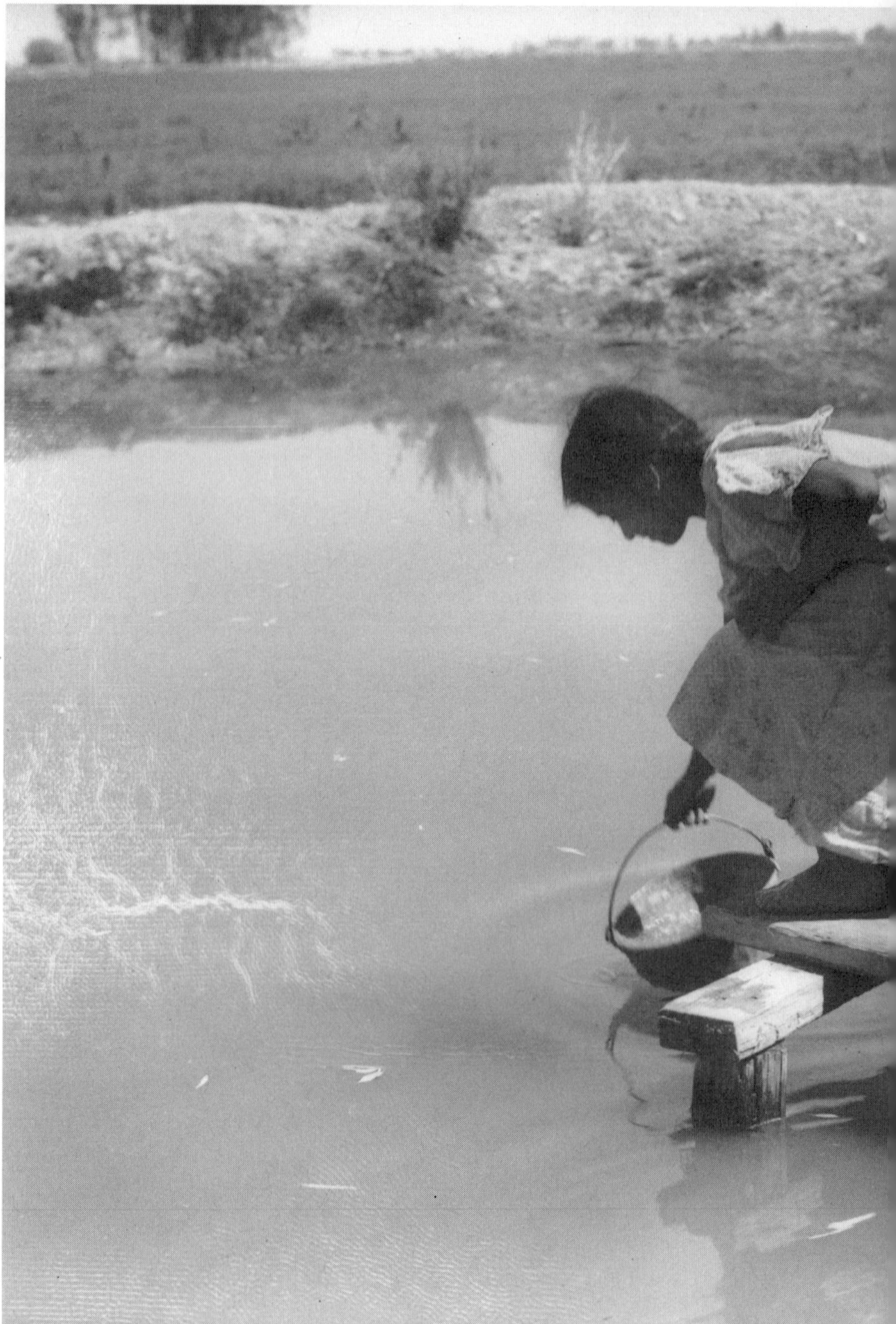

FIGURE 18. Dorothea Lange, *Drinking Water for Field Worker's Family.* Library of Congress, Prints & Photographs Division, FSA-OWI Collection, [LC-USF34-001619-C].

In the Imperial Valley Lange discovered quintessential representations of the "human erosion" of the dust bowl. The juxtaposition of Taylor and Lange's work sharpens the irony of the workers' situations. Taylor's narrative is scientific, its cool detachment sharpening its implicit criticism of the Imperial Valley. Lange's interviews, in contrast, are intimate, specific, and humanizing. In one photograph (figure 19), for example, the migrant mother is still smiling, the child standing tall in the doorway of their shelter, despite the unrelenting landscape around the makeshift dwelling.

According to Taylor, intensive, large-scale, and highly seasonal agriculture had "created in California the largest wage-earning class, proportionately, of any important agricultural state" (104). The result was "a large, landless, and mobile proletariat" (104). The sheer numbers of people involved were staggering: "Between 1935 and 1939 a full 300,000 persons of this class, or an average of above 6, 000 a month, were counted entering the borders of [California] by automobile" (110). The outlook for the new arrivals was bleak:

> Unlike the nineteenth century immigrants to the west,
> these migrants find the old West is gone. Land is limited
> and dear. It was capitalized in the days of Chinese immigration
> on the expectation of continued ample supplies of cheap
> labor. It must be watered, and the cost of irrigation is high.
> Its price is in the hundreds of dollars per acre, beyond the
> reach of propertyless refugees from plantation, midcontinent,
> plains, or dust bowl. (111)

In such passages, Taylor's voice is unblinkingly factual. He enunciates neither individuals nor landscape, only abstract forces that threaten human decency:

> The conditions of laborers who serve highly industrialized,
> highly specialized, highly seasonal agriculture are not easy.
> The succession of sharp harvest peaks—separated by hundreds
> of miles—requires mobile workers ready to follow the crops.
> But the insistence of demand for their labor to tend perishable
> products has no balance in security of employment. In California
> the fluctuations which employ three laborers at the peak in the
> fall leave two of them without jobs on farms in the spring. Hire
> and fire as needed is the rule. (111)

Taylor has no time to waste on protecting the feelings of the valley's elites. His report is sharp and clear: "At the conclusion of the pea harvest in one county the supervisors voted $2500 to fill the tanks of the pickers' cars with gasoline—enough to get them into the next county to avoid having to feed them" (112). The one time he quotes a local source it is to blandly cite a newspaper article that worried aloud about "the 'importation' of hordes of undesirable people and the creation of troublesome social problems" (112). Ten weeks later, he reports, the same paper ran the following ad: "Wanted—1000 cotton pickers for Imperial Valley, CA . . . $100 per hundred pounds, Colonists rates will be in effect on all railroads."

In contrast, Lange's interviews unleash the subjective voices of everyday Americans. She uses the workers' own words as captions to her images: "She: 'I want to go back to where we can live happy, live decent, and grow what we eat.' He: 'I've made my mistake and now we can't go back, I've got nothing to farm with.'" One displaced person lamented, "We trust in the Lord and don't expect much" (135). An unexpected result of Lange's inclusion of these voices is the exposure of the increasingly racialized nature of the migrants' worldview. Although the reader is meant to sympathize with the uprooted farmers, they say a number of unsettling things. Many underscore their "whiteness" and suggest that they should therefore be treated differently than black sharecroppers and Mexican laborers. "We ain't no paupers," one farmer tells Lange, "we hold ourselves to be white folks" (135). Lange recorded that one dust-bowl exile claimed, "The Mexican is *through* in Calif. The Americans have rooted them out" (160).

Although the book ends with an image of Ma Burnam, a sunbonneted older woman who represents conventional, time-honored agrarian myths of family and farming, the Imperial Valley photographs that precede it present a starker and more complicated story. One taken near Holtville in 1937 could have served to illustrate the book's subtitle, "human erosion" (figure 20). In this picture, Lange puts all of the techniques of landscape, technology, and portraiture that she learned in the Imperial Valley to profound use. As in other valley photographs, the image is overexposed to fade out the horizon and to wash tent fabric, desert sand, and sky together into one blinding continuum. The technique allows the black Fords to center the middle ground, but it is the contrasting shapes and tones of the garbage in the foreground that become the subject of the photograph. Humans are insignificant here both in terms of their size relative to the

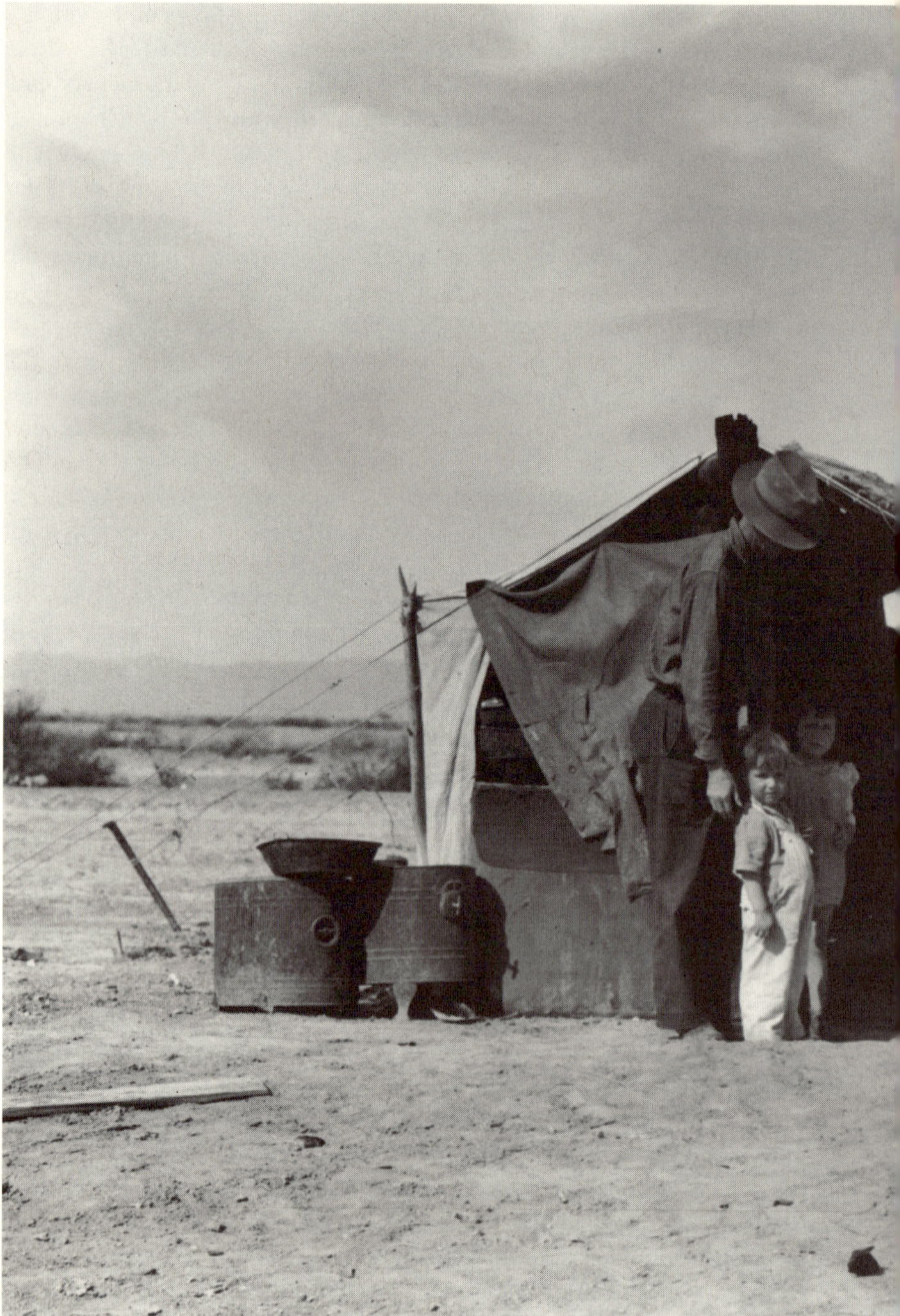

FIGURE 19. Dorothea Lange, *Neideffer Camp, Holtville, Imperial Valley, California*. Library of Congress, Prints & Photographs Division, FSA-OWI Collection, [LC-USF34-016251-C].

100

FIGURE 20.
Dorothea Lange,
*Refugee Families
Encamped Near
Holtville, California.*
Library of Congress,
Prints & Photographs
Division, FSA-OWI
Collection,
[LC-USF 34-16247-C].

| 101

FIGURE 21. Russell Lee, *Exhibit of Grapefruit at the Imperial County Fair, California*. Library of Congress, Prints & Photographs Division, FSA-OWI Collection, [LC-USF34-072165-D].

junk that frames them and their washed-out hues, which fade into the harsh landscape.

By the time *American Exodus* appeared in print, American readers were absorbed by the war effort and the book never experienced the sales and critical acclaim it deserved. The Imperial Valley's elites weathered the red storm of the thirties and turned their prodigious mythologizing powers toward the war effort. At the Imperial Country Fair in 1941, a photograph taken for the Office of War Information caught this remarkable image on film (figure 21). The enthusiastic, patriotic message is made entirely of citrus fruit. Such photographs quickly replaced those taken by the FSA as the government's use of image was put to the service of war. Like Lange's endless rows of peas, this picture of the grapefruit banner is an image of superabundance. The great national project of the war justified productivity; no critique is offered of the labor that went into its production.

During the forties, Dorothea Lange used her cameras and notebook to record the injustices of the Japanese internment. But she never returned to the Imperial Valley and thus never told the story of the Japanese tenant farmers who lived there. That valley story was left to Wakako Yamauchi, who began writing about her Imperial Valley girlhood in the 1960s, when she was finally able to confront the pain of internment through stories of 1930s desert isolation and loneliness.

5 "A Dying Reed by the River Bed"

| When I was young, the only stories I knew about Japanese people had to do with World War II. My mother used to tell us that in her San Gabriel elementary school class, the Japanese kids refused to salute the flag in the months leading up to the attack on Pearl Harbor. They knew, she implied, what was coming. My father, who was a good ten years older than my mother, remembered spending the morning of December 7, 1941, having breakfast in Mexicali, just across the border from his Imperial Valley home. When word came of the attack, he said that everyone, as if on signal, got up to pay their checks. Within an hour, a steady stream of stunned and silent Americans waited in a long line at the border, desperate to get home. During the next week, another long line of human beings clustered along the border—this time headed in the other direction—as Mexicans, unsure of their own futures as "aliens," waited to cross back into Mexico.

California was rife with such stories in the 1940s. Right after the attack, Anglo America was willing to believe just about anything. The Japanese on Hawaii had cut arrows in the cane fields to guide the bombers to their targets. Downed enemy pilots were found to be wearing American college class rings. State attorney general Earl Warren reported that the Japanese in California had embarked on "a sinister pattern of land ownership," certainly arranged to facilitate espionage.

To Anglo Americans, Japanese people suddenly seemed alien, cryptic, difficult to read. Culbert Olsen, governor of California in 1941, put it best. "You know," he said to a group of Japanese American journalists, "when I look out at a group of Americans of German or Italian descent, I can tell whether they are loyal or not. I can tell how they think... but it is impossible for me to do this with the inscrutable Orientals, and particularly with the Japanese" (Hansen and Mitson 29).

It was only much later that Japanese Americans got the chance to tell their own stories, to shed the mask of imposed inscrutability. They would then explore what it meant to be both Japanese and American, to be the only group of American citizens ever imprisoned en masse because of their ethnic heritage. One of the first to do this in fiction and drama was Wakako Yamauchi, a second-generation (Nisei) woman who grew up in the little town of Westmoreland, at the north end of the Imperial Valley, during the 1930s.

Yamauchi's experience of the Imperial Valley seemed to provide her a key to understanding postwar Nisei existence. Garrett Hongo has characterized Japanese Americans who shared Yamauchi's fate as carrying "an incredible burden of pain and disappointment" (Yamauchi 1). The prewar period of anti-Japanese racism and the humiliation of internment left many first-generation (Issei) immigrants "heartbroken and exhausted." But the Nisei were determined to move forward. "Who had time to reflect on the past?" Hongo asks, "on the camps? Who wanted to?" (2).

Silent, mysterious, almost passive—the desert could be described in terms very similar to those used to dehumanize Japanese Americans. One of the first Anglo Americans to see the Imperial Valley was struck by this quality of the Salton Basin, "Nothing is known of the country. I have never heard of a white man who has penetrated it."

Perhaps Wakako Yamauchi saw herself reflected back by the Imperial Valley, the unknown and impenetrable desert. Although she lived for many years in many other places—she was not a tenant farmer like her parents—and never returned to the desert after the war, the Imperial Valley stayed with her. It haunted her. In the dreams of one of her narrators, we see "the country kitchen of my childhood: furniture of raw unfinished wood, bare floors, sweaters on pegs, gray dishcloths drying on the sink rim, cosmic dust slowly sifting." Beyond the farmhouse windows, Yamauchi recalls, stretched the "desert, broken nearby with rows of furrowed earth" (42). "Am I the mother or am I the child," the narrator asks, "am I the caller or the called?" (42).

Yamauchi's memories of 1930s life in the Imperial Valley are rooted in a time that saw the end of legal immigration from Japan. In Japanese American families, the children were citizens while their parents were barred by law from obtaining the rights and responsibilities of being Americans. It was a volatile period in U.S-Japanese relations that culminated in the bombing of Pearl Harbor and the 1942 internment of "all persons of Japanese ancestry, both alien and non-alien." There is no other immigrant story like it in America.

When immigration from Japan began in the nineteenth century, neither the Japanese nor the Americans believed it would last long or have much of an effect. Unlike other groups, the Japanese came slowly and sporadically, driven by a different set of cultural assumptions and economic needs than those arriving from Eastern Europe and Italy. Although Japanese names appear in the California historical record as early as 1869, as a group they never reached the numbers of other foreign laborers like the Chinese. In the 1890s, only 2,039 Japanese people were living in the United States, as compared to 100,000 Chinese. The Japanese who emigrated looked at themselves as part of a long-standing tradition of people—called *dekasegi*—who left their country homes temporarily to seek employment to supplement agricultural income. As first-generation immigrant Yoshito Fuji remembered it, "I imagined the United States to be a good country with a lot of future prospects. I didn't have any deep thoughts, for I didn't intend to stay here a long time" (Sarasohn 23).

Some came because they had failed university entrance exams and wanted to study English in order to return to Japan and start international businesses. Others came because they were second sons in a system of primogeniture and were tired of being treated "small" in their home villages. Still others came as brides in arranged marriages, or to recover losses sustained in business in Japan. They came because a father or brother called them, because American farmers were said to live cleaner lives and didn't have to haul human feces from the cities to fertilize their crops.

They came on ships like the *America Maru*, the *Mongolia*, and the *Saibei Maru*, bound for San Francisco and Seattle. Many were inspired by a flurry of promotional literature that cast America as a golden land where a laborer's dollars were worth twice as much as Japanese yen. Pamphlets printed and distributed in Japan and titled "How to Succeed in America" and "Guide to Different Occupations in America" ran to more than thirty editions and told amazing success stories like that of George Shima, the famous "Potato King" of the Sacramento Delta, who had turned a failed university career into a multimillion dollar farming empire. Under the pressures of economic hardships in their local villages, and the lure of this tempting propaganda, the trickle of Japanese immigration to the United States in the nineteenth century turned into a flood.

By 1900, there were eleven emigration companies operating in Japan and a new kind of immigrant was heading to the Pacific Coast of the United States. Mostly young, and largely single, they were men intent on personal gain, on striking it rich before returning to the old country with a taste of America's celebrated freedom and perhaps a potato kingdom of their own. Some were peasants, forced out of Japan by the economic pressures of an economy in the process of transforming from a feudal to a capitalist system. But most were middle-class men looking for a nest egg to bring home to parents and in-laws.

As their numbers increased, and as they grew successful in turning poor, leased land into cash crops, some West Coast residents began to complain of a "Japanese Problem." The governments of Japan and the United States intervened in 1907 to halt further immigration into the United States by common laborers. Known as the "Gentleman's Agreement," the immigration bill gave the American president the power to eliminate "secondary immigration" by prohibiting Japanese workers from entering via Canada, Hawaii, and Mexico. By 1924, the passage of the Immigration Act had halted all Japanese immigration.

But the die was already cast. Because wages were low for farm laborers, and racist practices kept them out of higher paying jobs or actual farm ownership, Issei men were forced to stay much longer in America than they had planned. And the longer they stayed, the less likely they were to return to Japan. Many succumbed to what one Issei woman describes as the "Magic 3"—gambling, drinking, and prostitution. Among the oral histories of the Issei, this generation of male immigrants is famous for hard living, hard labor, and transience.

When the Gentleman's Agreement started to limit the number of men arriving from Japan, Japanese women began to make up the majority of those traveling to America. The practice of "picture brides"—marriages arranged through the exchange of photographs—began to flourish. The man's family in Japan would find what they considered a suitable marriage partner, complete the marriage ceremony without the groom, and send the bride over armed only with her new husband's picture and youthful hopes. As many as one in four Japanese women arriving in the 1910s was a picture bride.

By the end of World War I, the Gentleman's Agreement had given way to very uncivilized behavior on the part of the Americans. Grassroots racist organizations with glittering names like the Native Sons and Daughters of the Golden West and the American Legion argued that the Japanese were "not the stuff of which Americans can be made." They were bolstered by the wild accusations of the Hearst newspapers, which from 1906 to 1941 kept up a steady drumbeat of anti-Japanese rhetoric. Soon politicians took up the anti-Japanese cause. Running for reelection to the U.S. Senate in 1921, James D. Phelan of San Francisco adopted a no-nonsense approach. "Keep California White," his election banners read. In 1922, the Supreme Court ruled that the Japanese were "aliens ineligible to citizenship." Wakako Yamauchi was born in the Imperial Valley in 1924, the year the United States halted all immigration from Japan. A descendent of the Massachusetts Puritans, Henry Cabot Lodge, helped push the bill through Congress.

Eventually, it was land that took center stage in the controversy. Forced by anti-Japanese legislation and prejudice to put all their considerable skills to work in farm labor, more than half of Japanese immigrants had, by 1920, adopted agriculture as their ticket to economic and social freedom. Most lived in California, concentrated in twelve of the state's fifty-eight counties—in places like Cortez and Del Rey in the Central Valley, and Westmoreland in the Imperial Valley. At a time when a white laborer received from $1.75 to $2.00 per day, a Japanese worker could be hired for $1.25. Using a racist calculus based on the supposed smaller stature of the Japanese, the growers reckoned they needed about 50 cents less a day to subsist.

In spite of these hurdles, however, some Japanese laborers became expert farmers, and many eventually saved enough of their wages to buy or lease their own land. A 1909 government report estimated that Japanese farmers leased 25 percent of California's arable land. In Imperial County, Japanese farmers accounted for fifty-one farms totaling 3,348 acres in 1909.

On the face of it, this would seem like good news. The immigrant Japanese, despised by Anglos for their different ways, had at least not become a drain on the economy. They had not "taken away" high-skill, high-wage jobs from white workers and had, in fact, supported agriculture at a time when there were not enough laborers to meet the demands of modern, capitalistic farming. But in reality, America often hates a winner.

The authors of a 1937 WPA report on the state of Japanese farming in California attempted to explain the complex dynamics at work:

> The Japanese farmer of California is an inoffensive, industrious, and extremely frugal individual. The great question is whether he fits into American life. The points against him, strange as it may appear, are his virtues, that is, his tireless energy and highly economic method of living.
>
> The white farmer on the other hand, is used to and demands a better standard of life. Although not afraid of arduous toil, provided ultimate benefits are commensurate with effort expended, he nevertheless balks at the idea of continuous serf-like drudgery as practiced by his Japanese competitor. (WPA 66)

The bottom line was, wherever the Japanese engaged in agriculture, crop prices fell and rents rose. And most outrageous of all, "the original American tenants and settlers [were] forced to move away or take up other professions."

As a result of this climate of conspiracy and resentment, state governments intervened in the Japanese "crisis." In 1913 California passed the Alien Land Law, which stated that people who were ineligible for citizenship could not own property and could lease land for a maximum of three years. Similar measures were adopted in most of the western states. There were loopholes in the laws that the Japanese exploited; they purchased land in the names of minor children who were citizens, or used corporations with substantial Japanese minority interest. But the fact remained that there were fewer and fewer chances of becoming a Potato King.

Japanese immigrants came to the Imperial Valley at the height of this period, at the same time that Harold Bell Wright's *The Winning of Barbara Worth* was making the valley the locus of Anglo American dreams about reclamation and progress. The valley was ripe for cheap labor willing to work in nearly intolerable conditions. Despite Wright's millennial vision, whites did not flood into the area to realize their racial destinies. Instead, as noted, they balked "at the idea of continuous serf-like drudgery as practiced by [their] Japanese competitor[s]."

Wakako Yamauchi's father, Wasaku Nakamura, was one of the Japanese immigrants who *did* take up the desert's challenge. Like many Issei men, he had journeyed alone to America to (as one of Yamauchi's characters put it) "make money, go home, live like a king." Also like many such men, he married late, in his thirties. He traveled back to Japan to collect the wife he had married through an arrangement by their families in the Shimizu Prefecture. Yamauchi's mother, Hamako Machida, spent her first night in America—New Years Day 1920—in prison, awaiting the outcome of a government-mandated medical checkup.

We have no record what her mother thought when her father "took his bride to his 15 acres of leased desert farmland near the town of Westmoreland at the north end of the Imperial Valley." Perhaps her feelings were similar to those of a contemporary immigrant, Michiko Tanaka, when she first set eyes on her new Central Valley home in 1922: "The walls were plastered with pictures from magazines, the floors were dirt, and there was only one bed.... From the window I caught a glimpse of farmers in overalls shooting guns and I thought, 'What an ugly place'" (Kikumura 28). A Japanese visitor to the valley in those days recalled that the situation was terrible for many Japanese: "The houses where they lived were just like chicken coops, narrow and small, and looked like remodeled stables" (Sarasohn 75).

Wakako Yamauchi's stories about life in the Imperial Valley between the World Wars lays bare the duplicity of Anglo American claims regarding the "imperial" agrarian aspirations of Japanese immigrants. Through these tales, we gain an "inside" perspective on the true lives of immigrants that lie behind the sensational tales of infiltration and conspiracy circulated by Hearst's press and the Sons and Daughters of the Golden West. Behind the hard-to-read faces of the Issei and their children were layers of stories—why they came to America, how they came, what they did when they got there. Yamauchi's stories hint at a deep and complex past, one filled with love and affection, divorce and abortions, disgrace and obedience, greed and "fatalism." Mostly they tell the story of two generations caught between two nations, two standards of civility, and two very different landscapes.

Some of the stories are about people left trapped in the desert by the death of the family patriarch, like Akiko Nagata in "In Heaven and Earth." The young narrator of this tale calmly reports the details of her father's death: "He'd fallen one night from a catwalk bridging the All American Canal.... They'd found him in the morning caught in a large tumbleweed wedged in some rocks, the muddy Colorado water lapping gently around his face" (25). The dangers of the laborer's life, the contingencies of weather and markets are what shape the lives of young Nisei like Akiko, not the cunning plots to manipulate the market cited in the WPA report.

The Japanese in Yamauchi's stories are very much at the mercy of the elements and the seasons, especially in the Lower Colorado Desert. A typical season for a Japanese farmer in the Imperial Valley began in May with the hauling of tons of chicken manure, which then had to be worked into the soil:

> Planting started in late September: tomatoes, squash, cantaloupe. All during the winter months, it was thinning the seedlings, weeding, building brush covers for them, repairing the covers after a storm, and starting the smudge pots to ward off the frost. In early spring, it was harvesting the crops. By May, after the broiling sun had reduced the plants to dry twigs, the plowing began. Then the land was flooded to start the weeds and fallen seeds growing, after which there was another plowing to destroy the sprouts, and once again fertilizing, furrowing, and preparing the land for late-September planting. (32)

The process was labor-intensive and minimally rewarding. "At best," Yamauchi recalled, "the entire process kept us alive and clothed." As year followed year, Japanese immigrants in the Imperial Valley moved "surely with the seasons." Nearly all hoped for the miracle that "would lift us up to Japan."

Children often alternated days at school, with one child working in the family's field while another attended classes. It was a precarious and disenfranchised existence. Land leases like Yamauchi's father's "were for three years, usually two, so the Japanese farmers and their families were always on the move, like desert Nomads" (225).

Sometimes the move was only five or ten miles from the site of their last lease. There they would choose a dusty corner of their parcel and set up shop again. Another valley Issei, Juhei Kono, recalled that "in the Imperial Valley of California. . . . [when] their land lease expired, [Japanese people] had a horse pull their house and move it on to another field to work" (Sarasohn 75).

Within this shifting and uncertain world, the Japanese of the Imperial Valley forged a tight community. Yamauchi's stories tell of Japanese neighbors and townspeople, Buddhist temple members, ladies' auxiliary, and summers spent at Terminal Island on the San Pedro Harbor when the desert got too hot for planting. Whites rarely intrude into Yamauchi's desert world (figure 22).

The immigrants' lives are, however, split along gender and generational lines. Mothers dream of Japan and fathers don't want to talk about it. Sons and daughters learn English at school and speak imperfect Japanese; they read *Photoplay* and *Modern Screen* and perm their hair. Issei parents try their best to instill their children with Japanese values and social mores, but the pressures of life in a racist country and desert landscape take their toll, especially on the women.

There is Mrs. Oka, in "And the Soul Shall Dance," whose "taste for liquor was a step into the realm of men." She rolls her own Bull Durham cigarettes and bears the bruises of her husband's beatings. To the young narrator of the story, Mrs. Oka appears "strange." When she sees her at the story's end, picking desert flowers at twilight while skipping to an old Japanese song, she can only comment, "the picture of her imagined grandeur was lost to me, but the delusion that transformed a bouquet of tattered petals and sandy leaves, and the loneliness of the desert twilight into a fantasy that brought such joy and abandon made me stir with discomfort" (24).

There is also the narrator's mother, who "spoke often of returning to Japan, of smelling again the piney woods, tasting the exquisite fruits, of seeing her beloved sisters." The stories she tells her children about Japan take on the aura of "a flashback in the movies—misty, wavering, ethereal." In telling them, "her beautiful eyes would grow soft" (33).

The men who surround these first-generation women, the husbands and unmarried laborers who crowd into their houses to eat their cooking and drink their sake, bury their longing for Japan in days of work and nights of card playing. The farmers have "squinty eyes" from laboring in the sun. Men of few words, they respond to their wives' longing for home with "wide-open, no horizon, uninhabitable desert silence" (47).

Shadowing them are other men, men who catch the eyes of the yearning mothers and isolated daughters. They are the father's bachelor friends, migrants who follow "the crops along the length of California, cutting lettuce in Dinuba, harvesting grapes in Fresno, plums, peaches, and finally strawberries in Oceanside and those little-known places—Vista, Escondido, Encinitas." The Nisei daughter in "That Was All" relates how these men "spent their money as they got it—drinking, gambling, carousing—until at the southernmost end of the state, they looked for us and stayed two or three months eating my mother's cooking, drinking my father's wine" (48).

Yamauchi also writes of another class of men who settle down to farming one plot. Suzuki-San, in "That Was All" lives alone, but manages to cut a gallant figure despite his poverty. There is something romantic about the way he lives on a ranch some thirty miles from his nearest Japanese neighbors, "in a treeless landscape of sand and tumbleweed." The narrator is drawn to him because his home seems "more desolate than where we lived, maybe because where we lived there was a mother and father and a child, and where Suzuki-san lived, there was only him and two bleak structures,

FIGURE 22. Leo Hetzel, *Japanese Armistice Day, Imperial Valley, 1928.* Imperial County Historical Society.

| 115

a kitchen and a bedroom, and the land beyond this complex and ranch was untouched from year to year, century to century" (47).

For the younger generation, the lure of individualism, of American progress and entrepreneurialism over and against Japanese traditionalism and communalism, seems to imbue such men with romantic power. Most dangerous of all to the stability of Issei life are the Kibei, Japanese children born in America and reared in Japan. They return to the life of American farm labor with a certain romantic detachment, an urbane skepticism that seems to leave them unsullied by the labor that subsumes the Issei husbands and fathers.

In "Songs My Mother Taught Me," the mother is attracted to Yamada-san, a Kibei laborer who works for the family for a short time. The father dislikes Yamada-San's cockiness and his familiarity with his wife, and soon turns him out. When the wife meets up with him again on a Terminal Island vacation, he somehow comes to represent to her an affirmation of her image of Japan "—the haunting flutes, the cherry blossoms, the poetry, the fatalism" (35). Yamauchi's story implies that an illicit union between the lonely Issei mother and romantic Kibei drifter results in an unwanted child, which the unsuspecting Issei husband assumes is his own. The story ends tragically when the mother drowns the baby while washing him on a hot and lifeless desert afternoon, perhaps because the child crystallizes her realization that "the dreams of returning to Japan were shattered." "Through the eyes of a younger man," the narrator tells us, "she had glimpsed what might have been, could never and would never be again" (38).

Yamauchi's family left the Imperial Valley in 1940 when an earthquake measuring close to seven on the Richter scale rocked the valley's north end. Five people were killed and more than a half a million dollars in damage reported. "The spring of the great Imperial Valley earthquake was the culmination of my father's farming career—his biggest failure," Yamauchi wrote. Leaving behind "one hundred and forty acres of lettuce nobody wanted" (238), her family joined other Japanese farmers in "a small exodus to Oceanside" (228).

In Oceanside, a town on the coast north of San Diego, Yamauchi's mother opened a boarding house for itinerant laborers. Wakako began attending Oceanside High School. Family friends settled nearby and went to work hauling produce. Although they were dirt poor, there was still a community feel about the place. With the cool ocean breezes and more regular harvest seasons, the Nakamura family probably thought they were done once and for all with the desert. But two years later, the actions of Imperial

Japan led to a second, forced isolation in desert solitude. The desert this time was located at the Poston internment camp along the banks of the Colorado River in western Arizona.

Internment blindsided both the Issei and their American-born children. Immediately after the attack, Issei assets were frozen, and their auto insurance policies were cancelled; many Nisei were discharged from their jobs without explanation. Acting swiftly to quell imaginary rampaging Japanese saboteurs, the FBI took into custody some fifteen hundred Issei community leaders and suspected pro-Japan sympathizers. The West Coast was declared a military zone, called the Western Defense Command (WDC).

On February 19, 1942, Franklin Roosevelt signed Executive Order 9066, which authorized the rounding up and jailing of all Japanese aliens and American citizens of Japanese lineage within the WDC. Shortly thereafter, the president created the War Relocation Authority (WRA), a civilian/governmental agency assigned to "processing" those who fell under the edict of Executive Order 9066. By March a curfew was in place that restricted Japanese American travel to the hours between 6:00 a.m. and 8:00 p.m. and to within five miles of their place of residence. Those living near airfields and factories were turned out of their homes.

In the spring of 1942, Japanese Americans in the Imperial Valley were selling everything they owned for a few cents on the dollar. Before abandoning their homes for good, many burned books and even family photos, fearing they would somehow be used as "evidence" against them. "Books were especially difficult to burn," one survivor remembers, "so we had to tear pages piece by piece" (Sarasohn 162). Those who had Kendo martial arts gear buried it in their yards, believing authorities would mistake it for military hardware.

Between March and August, when the "relocation" was completed, the WRA rounded up more than 110,000 people. They were taken by bus or train to hastily constructed "Assembly Centers" in old fair grounds, race tracks, and Civilian Conservation Corps camps. From there, the prisoners were transferred to one of ten prison camps scattered across the western half of the United States. With the exception of the Jerome and Rohwer camps, which were situated in southeastern Arkansas, the camps were established in remote, desert locations. As most were not yet ready when the internees arrived, the Japanese were set to the task of building their own prisons. Forty thousand of these prisoners of war were children.

The two largest camps—Poston and Gila River—were located in Arizona and together housed thirty-five thousand internees. Wakako Yamauchi and her family were sent to Poston, a compound on the eastern shore of the Colorado River, about a hundred miles from her old Imperial Valley home. When Poston held its full complement of detainees, it became the third largest city in Arizona. Ironically, Poston was located on the Colorado River Indian Reservation, and the powers-that-be decided to turn over its running to John Collier, commissioner of Indian Affairs. Jack Matusoka's cartoon drawings from Poston show that this irony was not lost on the inmates. In one image, Matsuoka sketched a truckload of detainees being driven through the desert. As one of the figures in the truck waves to two Native men, another comments, "How! He looks like your Cousin Taro." Matsuoka captions his drawing, "Greetings from the original Americans" (figure 23).

For three years Yamauchi lived yet another desert existence in this makeshift city, along with many of the valley's Japanese residents. Mildred Ota, one-time Calexico High valedictorian and UCLA graduate was there. So was Robert J. Maeda, originally from El Centro, who would later become a professor of art history at Brandeis. Poston even became home to modernist sculptor Isamu Naguchi, perhaps the most famous Japanese American intellectual of the period.

Life at Poston brought the desert right into the homes of the Japanese internees. In her memoir of life in the camp, Mrs. Hanayo Inouye remembered that "dust was one of our biggest problems. However tight we shut the windows and doors, the dust came in the house and all over the inside" (Sarasohn 196). Weeds sprouted between the floorboards of the cabins, and Naguchi summed up the feelings of many when he said, "Here, time has stopped, and nothing is of any consequence" (155).

The desert around the camps threw the dislocation of the internees into sharp relief, providing a sort of material touchstone for their psychological alienation. Memoirs of the internment abound with descriptions of the harsh landscapes. Yoshiko Uchida's first view of Topaz, in the Utah desert, is typical: "There no trees or grass or growth of any kind, only stumps of dry skeletal greasewood" (Uchida 105). The feelings behind her matter-of-fact description of the desert are embodied in her mother's *tanka* written in the camp:

> Banished to this
> Desert land,
> I cherish the
> Blessing of the sky.
> (Uchida 121)

FIGURE 23. Jack Matsuoka, *Greetings from the First Americans*. From *Camp II, Block 211: Daily Life in an Internment Camp*. San Francisco: Japan Publications, 1974.

Jack Matsuoka's cartoons counter the shock of desert alienation with humor. "Before we could move into our new home," Matsuoka reported, "we had to move the scorpions out" (28). Like other internees, Matsuoka remembered most of all the dust: "Here's dust in your mouth. An Arizona dust storm is something you can't run away from. No matter whether is comes by day—when you can at least see it on its way—or by night, all you can do is bear it and try not to eat too much dust" (72). One side of the camp fence was never finished. It faced the desert, however, and as Matsuoka pointed out,

"A Dying Reed by the River Bed"

FIGURE 24. Fred Clark, *Jim Morikawa Sprinkling in an Attempt to Settle the Dust.* Poston Internment Camp, 1942. Courtesy of The Bancroft Library. University of California, Berkeley.

"nobody would try to go too far in that direction" (122). There is a bleak photograph from Poston in this period showing camp members leaning against a dusty desert wind as the man in the foreground in vain tries to sprinkle down the dirt around the barracks with a garden hose (figure 24). As Uchida had testified, there are no trees, grass, or shrubs, and really no horizon. Only the black tarpaper shacks interrupt the continuous line of earth and sky.

Despite their predicament, some internees managed to occasionally find solace in the desert's beauty. Yoshiko Uchida remembers early evening as "a peaceful time of day." At dusk,

> the sand retained the warmth of the sun, and the moon rose from behind dark mountains with the kind of clear brilliance seen

only in a vast desert sky. We often took walks along the edge of the camp, watching sunsets made spectacular by the dusty haze and waiting for the moon to rise in the darkening sky. It was one of the few things to look forward to in our life at Topaz. (Uchida 112)

Such positive experiences were, however, rare. Internment, desert alienation, and near-forced labor turned camp life into an eerie reiteration of the Japanese immigrants' time in California before the war, complete with low wages and backbreaking work. Already psychologically displaced, the prisoners' social organization, set up by the WRC, also worked to exacerbate intergenerational strife. Conflict between the Issei, Kibei, and Nisei reached a fever pitch early on at Poston, where the traditional authority of the Issei was undermined by the camp organization, which put Nisei in charge. The first major strike erupted in November 1942, just a few months after the internees had arrived. It was sparked by "the arrest of two men accused of beating a suspected *innu* or informer." The situation worsened in 1943 when the government reversed its position on Japanese Americans serving in the military and sent recruiters to the camps. Armed with the now-infamous army and WRC questionnaires, the recruiters asked the prisoners, "Will you swear unqualified allegiance to the United States of America and forswear any form of allegiance to the Japanese emperor . . . ?" Pushing tensions further, the follow-up question was, "Are you willing to serve in the armed forces of the United States on combat duty, wherever ordered?"

Yoshiko Uchida explains the conflicting emotions stirred up by these questions. "Since, at the time, the Issei were by law classified 'aliens ineligible for citizenship,'" the first question basically "would have left them without a country." In terms of the second, "many Nisei men felt they could not answer yes . . . until their civil rights were restored." Some buried their resentment and answered yes to both queries. Many others answered "no" to both on principle, thereby earning the label "no-no boys." Like camp organization, the questionnaires fed into the already existing battles between the generations and new, emerging social factions.

All these aspects of desert exile touched Wakako Yamauchi's life at Poston. Already a budding author, the camp forced her talent into the open. She went to work on the *Poston Chronicle*, a paper printed by and for internees. There she met Hisaye Yamamoto, who had written stories and columns for the Japanese American press before the war. Poston taught Yamauchi the power of storytelling, how it could help to manage memory and desire in a time of hardship.

Yamauchi herself earned early release from the camp by agreeing to work in a candy factory in Chicago. Internment, however, spelled doom for her family. She would never see her father again. He died of a heart attack at Poston before she had a chance to reunite with him.

For Japanese Americans, neither the American dream nor the American landscape would ever be the same after Poston, Manzanar, Tule Lake, and other internment centers. Poston changed forever Wakako Yamauchi's memories of her youth in the Lower Colorado. In her Imperial Valley stories, written in the 1960s, the deserts emerge from her memory as a central symbol of the Nisei's collective quest to deal (often quietly and privately) with the trauma of the past. In these stories and her most famous play, *And the Soul Shall Dance*, which she adapted from an earlier short story, Yamauchi exploits the real-world tension between the tenant farmlands of the Japanese immigrants and the harsh landscape of the Lower Colorado Desert in the 1930s. She channels these tensions into explorations of her second desert exile of the 1940s.

The Imperial Valley desert functions as a multivalent symbol in Yamauchi's stories—at once a figure of alienation (especially the kind of alienation felt by the Issei), and an emblem of imagination and escape. In the first case, desert imagery underscores the plight of an immigrant generation whose dreams and hard work butt up constantly against the desert's unyielding reality. "What is this compulsion to commune with this nothing land?" one of Yamauchi's characters asks. It is a question that could stand for the angst of a whole generation.

In a particularly revealing exchange from *And the Soul Shall Dance*, Yamauchi dramatizes how the Imperial Valley came to represent the archetypal Japanese immigrant experience. A Nisei daughter, Masako Murata, reads to her mother from a schoolbook. "I love this story," she exclaims, "Mama, this is about people like us—settlers—it's about the prairie. We live in a prairie, don't we?" When her mother asks if "prairie" means "desert," Masako answers yes. The dialogue that follows underscores the irony of the Imperial Valley's Japanese immigrants' story within the larger progressive myth of coming to America:

> **Hana:** [looking at the bleak landscape]: We live in a prairie.
> **Masako:** It's about the hardships and the floods and droughts and how they have nothing but each other.
> **Hana:** We have nothing but each other. But these people... they're white people.

Masako: Sure, Mama. They come from the east. Just like
you and Papa...
Hana: We come from the far far east. That's different.
White people are different from us.
Masako: I know that. How come they don't write books about us...?
Hana: Because we're nobodies here. (181–82)

In the 1930s, the Imperial Valley was being touted as the last best place, the place of dreams. The reality, as Yamauchi remembers it, was quite different. When the "inland empire" betrays her and her family, the young Nisei girl escapes into books:

Masako: If I didn't read these, there'd be nothing for me.
Hana: Some of the things you read you are never going to know.
Masako: I can dream though. (182)

While the Imperial Valley's alkaline farmlands were less than inspiring, the surrounding desert could be a surprising boon to the imagination. In many of Yamauchi's stories, the desert's tempting and symbolic combination of imagination and memory serves as an ironic counterpoint to lives constrained by the soul-numbing routine of irrigation agriculture on marginal lands. Kimi, a dying woman reflecting back on her life in "The Boatman on Toneh River," recalls how the desert finally won her over: "Though you may not believe it, I've found something here in this arid desert that is gentle and sweet too" (43). In "That Was All," Yamauchi's narrator—like John C. Van Dyke and Jefferson Worth before her—wanders out into the desert at twilight in search of life's meaning:

> I wandered around looking for—I don't know what—maybe some indication that someone had been here before me and left something for me, and finding nothing, I stood by the fine pure sand the winds had pushed against a shrub and mused that it was possible I was the first person who had ever been on this particular mound of sand and put my shoe to that dust that began with creation and then my hand and then my cheek, and then my hair and finally rolled myself on it and fell asleep. (47)

Like most of Yamauchi's protagonists, this girl is Nisei, caught between her parents' love for Japan, its manners and traditions, and her own budding fascination with all things American. The desert offers a neutral territory where she can explore her feelings and a vantage point from which to critically examine both the traditional and the "American" way of life.

In other stories, the desert is figured as memory, escape, and longing. One of Yamauchi's earliest published stories, also called "And the Soul Shall Dance," is framed as the memory of a young female protagonist named Masako. Her desire to tell her tale can be read as a go-ahead for the release of all the Nisei's pent up anxiety about the past. "It's all right to talk about it now" (19), the narrator assures us in the story's first line.

Set in the mid-thirties, "And the Soul Shall Dance" follows a season in the lives of an unnamed Japanese immigrant family and their neighbors, the Okas. The Okas are childless and Mr. Oka is on his second marriage. His wife is a much younger woman who is unhappy in the desert and longs for Japan. Until their bathhouse burns down unexpectedly, the narrator's family does not interact much with the Okas.

The story explores the emergence of the narrator's voice as she witnesses the decline of one Issei woman into madness and the Americanization of another. It is the Lower Colorado Desert that gives young Masako perspective on the lives of the immigrant Japanese around her. "An alkaline road, a stretch of grease wood, tumbleweed, and white sand" separate her from the "strange" Okas (19). The loss of the bathhouse—a figure of both tradition and the progressive, life-giving power of water in this desert—forces the family to confront their own alienation by thrusting them symbolically deeper into the desert of the Oka's lives.

As the narrator's family is forced to interact with the Okas, using their bathhouse until their own can be rebuilt, Yamauchi foregrounds the presence of dust and dirt and the seeming inability of the family to "get clean" without its traditional bathhouse. As soon as the narrator's younger brother steps from the bath, his "feet are already sandy" (20).

With the arrival of Oka's daughter, Kiyoko-san, the story shifts to a coming-of-age tale that turns on the Americanization of the Japanese girl and its effect on the two families. For Mr. Oka, Kiyoko's arrival is a punishment. Relatives in the old country have sent the girl to America to get her off their hands. "If they knew," Mr. Oka says of his Japanese relations, "if they only knew how it was here" (21).

The two girls, Nisei and Kibei, however, become fast friends. Walking to and from school, Masako coaches Kiyoko on the proper pronunciation of English ls and rs. Within a few months, the fifteen-year-old Kibei girl has become a model of Americanization: "With her permanent wave, her straight black hair became tangles of frantic curls, between her textbooks she carried copies of *Modern Screen* and *Photoplay*" (23). As Kiyoko steps "gingerly over the white peaks of alkaline crust" (23), we witness the figurative ease by which she negotiates Anglo American culture.

In contrast, as autumn wears into winter in the valley, Mrs. Oka drifts further and further from reality and back toward the Japan of her dreams. The narrator's own unease at witnessing the assimilation of Kiyoko and the deterioration of Mrs. Oka causes her to seek solace in desert solitude: "Evenings were longer now, and when my mother's migraines drove me from the house in unbearable self-pity, I would take walks in the desert" (24). She lays on the "white sand and trie[s] to disappear" (24), wishing she could fit into Anglo America as easily as Kiyoko has. Instead, she somehow finds herself drawn to Japan. The Japanese popular songs Mrs. Oka sings as she walks in the desert in the evening picking flowers bring disturbingly exotic colors to the drab landscape, but these only sharpen Masako's growing passion for the desert's spareness and certainty:

> Red Lips
> Press against a glass
> Drink the green wine
> And the soul shall dance.
> (24)

Although the narrator claims that Mrs. Oka's "imagined grandeur" is lost to her, she admits that "the delusion that transformed a bouquet of tattered petals and sandy leaves, and the loneliness of the desert twilight into a fantasy that brought such joy and abandon made me stir with discomfort" (24). These are desert optics of a different kind from those of John Van Dyke. Like Yoshido Uchida at Topaz, Masako is enticed by the desert's "delusion," its powerful evocation of memory and desire.

In 1977, Yamauchi created a dramatic version of *And the Soul Shall Dance*. The play strengthens the desert's ambivalent symbolic role in the Nisei imagination. In the drama, the Lower Colorado is always felt just offstage, representing the margins of the material, social world. The final scene's stage directions highlight the minimalism of the setting: "Exterior, desert. There is at least one shrub, a tumbleweed, maybe." The desert functions as a plain, drab backdrop, a reflection of the washed-out interiors of the Japanese tenant farmhouses in which the dramatic action unfolds. Here and there, splashes of color and sound—kimonos from the old country, wind chimes (*furin*), or snatches of popular songs on a Victrola—alleviate the monotony. But the desert is mostly an extension of the immigrants' drab existence. Visually, the play challenges viewers to make sense of the desert setting, to judge the human qualities needed to redeem it. By thus seeking to open the audience's eyes and ears, Yamauchi's later version of the Imperial Valley coming of age story functions as a kind of Noh drama, drawing on music and dance to create a desert tone poem.

Set in 1935, *And the Soul Shall Dance* revisits the lives of the Murata family and their neighbors, the Okas. While the circumstances of the two families are the same, Mrs. Oka appears much more sophisticated here—she has studied the classics and was "almost *natori*," that is, almost a college graduate. As in the story, the play turns on the anticipated arrival of Mr. Oka's only child, Kiyoko, born to his first wife and raised in Japan, her conflicts with her stepmother, and her "Americanization" thanks to Masako's guidance. By making Mrs. Oka more complex (and Hana, the narrator's mother, more understanding), Yamauchi puts the women's perspective at the center of the desert fable.

The play begins with a bathhouse smoldering offstage. While it is Masako who accidentally set it ablaze, the fault is not her's alone. Yamauchi is careful to avoid having the play descend into a simple allegory about the dangers of abandoning tradition by stressing that the desert valley has played a role in the razing of custom: "This kind of weather dries everything," Murata announces, "[it] just takes a spark to make a bonfire."

Again, the Murata family is thus forced into greater social intercourse with the neighboring Okas, who offer to share their bath during the repairs. Suddenly in close proximity, the Muratas learn a great deal about the Okas—how Mr. Oka has fled a life of apprentice labor in Japan, how his first wife died, and how he is expecting his daughter to arrive from Japan. They also learn more about Mrs. Oka, who is rumored to be *kitchigai*—insane. As it turns out, Emiko Oka is a talented, educated woman whose madness results from her longing for Japan and the physical abuse she suffers at the hands of her husband. These details are much more than simple exposition, for the deep, untold lives of the Japanese immigrants are part of the play's revealing. They, as Masako points out, have never had a storyteller. "They don't write books about us," she says.

On the first evening at the Oka's bath, Masako brings along the Victrola as a friendly gesture, and she and Emiko connect over Japanese popular songs from the past. Emiko dances, Noh-like, in the window of the farmhouse, perhaps mimicking the pantomimes of the traditional Japanese

Kyojo-mono plays (mad woman pieces). Yamauchi, however, reinterprets the customary movements of the traditional drama to fit the earthly and historical motivations of the real-life Japanese experience of the Imperial Valley. It is the Nisei girl who witnesses the Noh dances through the window; it is her confusion and discomfort that conditions the viewers' understanding of Emiko's movements.

Like the short story, the dramatic version of *And the Soul Shall Dance* ends with Masako coming to terms with Kiyoko's assimilation and Mrs. Oka's madness. But in the play, Yamauchi holds in tension the material conditions of the Japanese immigrant experience (hard work and longing) with the seductive temptation to escape into the desert/imagination. The action concludes with Masako offering to close an irrigation gate for her father, who has come in from his long day of labor without having completed this significant task. It is something she's never offered to do before, and perhaps prefigures her growing adaptation to the hard work of a real Imperial Valley existence, her relinquishing of the illusory American life depicted in *Photoplay*. In moral terms, the Nisei daughter has grown into responsibility during the course of the play and has accepted her desert solitude.

But the play does not end with the characters' actions. It concludes—again, in the Noh tradition—with a visual image, to "open the eyes" of the audience to the desert. Yamauchi's stage directions call for the final scene to be done in pantomime, against a sparse desert set, with a few words sung in Japanese. Emiko appears in tableau against the sand and scrub, wearing "a beautiful kimono tied loosely at her waist." As Masako watches, the light slowly fades on the scene, "and the image of her forlorn form remains etched on the retina." As the curtain falls, the viewer is left with the impression of a photographic negative: Masako framed by the Imperial Valley Desert. It is a haunting darkroom image of postwar Nisei memory and desire. A story told by a woman who lived a Lower Colorado desert life in two dimensions—as a local farm girl and as an exiled outsider.

6 *Travesías*

> Entre las dos Californias
> quiero construir un puente,
> para que quando tú quieras,
> te pases del sur al norte,
> caminando libremente
> no como liebre del monte.
>
> —Gina Valdés, untitled poem,
> *Puentes y Fronteras*

| *Caminando libremente*—walking freely across two Californias, urban and rural, Anglo and Latino. In the Imperial Valley, it is not so much the bridge that beckons, but the passage itself. Trekking north from Baja to Alta California is a *travesía*, a crossing. I once saw firsthand what that means in the Lower Colorado Desert.

In 1969, I witnessed César Chávez leading a UFW march through my hometown of Brawley. I was in elementary school and the doors of the school had been locked against the marchers. Our teacher told us to stay away from the windows, but I couldn't resist sneaking over to watch. Chávez was flanked by brown berets, the Black Panthers of the Chicano/a movement, and the group strode down my town's main boulevard with great determination.

I didn't know it then, but the protest Chávez was leading was a symbolic reenactment of something called the *perigrenaje*, a term in Chicano/a culture that refers to the great (and continuing) migration of Mexican people into and out of the United States. It is at once a ritual of remembrance and affirmation. To walk the perigrenaje is to recall the suffering of all those who have walked those many miles before, as well as of those who perished in the desert crossing. To walk the perigrenaje is also to reaffirm the right of Mexican presence on this land, even if it is called the United States. It is to step to the cadence of these lines from poet and critic Gloria Anzaldúa:

> This land was Mexican once
> was Indian always . . .
>   And will be again.
>   (Anzaldúa 91)

Imperial Valley storytelling, from a Mexican perspective, entails a complex evocation of the perigrenaje. Mexican tales of this impossible land are always tales of two Californias—one a forbidding desert landscape where immigrants are forced to tread amid an alien culture, the other a "frontier" (*frontera* in Spanish suggests not only a border but a horizon and hope) where Mexican nationals have established posturban, postmodern, and postborder cities like Tijuana and Mexicali. In these places it is Mexican Spanish, not Castilian or English, that is the lingua franca. César Chávez's own life story, in fact, traces the outlines of these parallel narrative trajectories in the Imperial Valley and its adjacent borderlands. For Chávez not only led marches and strikes here, but spent his formative years in this irrigated desert valley.

The Chávez family's perigrenaje began in 1888 when César's grandfather fled the injustices of the Mexican hacienda system and settled in the Arizona Territory. Chávez would relate how the "family farm started three years before Arizona became a state." Although he was born in Yuma, Arizona, Chávez went to school in California, and it was there that he first felt the sting of racism. He started school in Oxnard, in segregated classrooms, and when his family moved to the Imperial Valley, he found education there even more humiliating: "The school in Brawley . . . was worse than the one in Oxnard. They wouldn't let us speak Spanish. If we did we were supposed to sit on a wooden bench in the back" (Levy 65).

As he worked the Imperial Valley's fields, Chávez also experienced firsthand the strange racial and economic hierarchies that render manual labor in this region so degrading. At the age of twelve, he "worked right alongside the men thinning cantaloupes in Brawley for a Japanese-American grower," who was "very difficult to work for, just [a] slave driver." Chávez recalled that most field laborers "preferred to work for the big companies where supervision wasn't that strict, but after those jobs were filled, there was no place to go except the Japanese Americans, who always paid a nickel less" (Levy 70).

Chávez's recollections of the 1940s valley stand in stark contrast to the storytelling tradition of Wakako Yamauchi and reveal how valley stories play off of one another. There is always another point of view, another story, another storyteller. "After Pearl Harbor," Chávez remembered,

> when the Japanese were relocated by the U.S. government. The Mexican workers rejoiced that the Japanese were put in internment camps just because the Japanese worked them so hard. In Brawley, people were celebrating. When I look back, I think it was an awful thing for the workers to have done, but to them it was like liberation. (Lovy 64)

In a way, Mexican American storytelling in the Imperial Valley emerged from this brief and painful liberation.

"Free" from Japanese overseers, and with Anglo American agricultural labor decimated by war and the draft, Mexican laborers grew to dominate the workforce in the Imperial Valley. In 1953, from one-half to four-fifths of agricultural laborers in the valley were Mexican. Two years later, more than 400,000 Mexican nationals were at work in U.S. fields (Galarza 25).

By the end of the first postwar decade, stories like those embedded in the life history of César Chávez were becoming common to a whole generation of Mexican immigrants and their American-born children. For many, the Imperial Valley would offer a narrative starting point, its irrigated desert one of the most recognizable "places" in the Mexican American West. As Latino/a writers and intellectuals in the 1950s began to enunciate an emergent Mexican American identity, several found that the Imperial Valley served well as a figure for the complex relationships Mexican Americans experienced between self and place and labor in their new country.

The valley's near-mythic status in Mexican American storytelling was established in print in 1959 when José Antonio Villarreal published *Pocho*, considered by many to be the first Mexican American novel. Richard Rubio, the *pocho* of the novel's title, is born "near Brawley, in the Imperial Valley, at a place where a dry creek met a tributary of the Canal del Alamo" (28). Richard's journey of self-discovery concerning what it means to be pocho—not quite Mexican, not quite American—pivots on his Imperial Valley birth to parents who were "a part of the great exodus that came of the Mexican Revolution" (15). Villareal describes the Imperial Valley's Mexican migrant population as a "bewildered people" who were "insensitive to the fact that even though they were not stopped, they were not really wanted." The story of their migration to the United States is cast in mythic terms, touching on the dream that had lured immigrants to the Imperial Valley since the time of Anza: "It was the ancient quest for El Dorado and so they moved onward, west to New Mexico and Arizona and California" (16).

Pocho opens in Mexico, with Richard's father being expelled by the ruling-party Caranzistas for murder. Juan Rubio is a follower of Pancho Villa and a self-confident man who views life through a revolutionary prism of racial and class hierarchy. When Villa is assassinated, Juan Rubio finally gives up all hope of returning to Mexico and settles in California a changed man. He stops drinking and gambling, learns to be "discreet in his love affairs," and finds a "new respect" for his wife. Richard Rubio's birth in the irrigated desert represents the symbolic domestication of the first generation of Mexicans born in the United States. These new Mexican Americans would come to believe that many of the traditional ways were "pura mierda" (pure shit), and that they could never be "wholly Mexican again" (63).

Like many valley storytellers before him, Villarreal's description of the landscape surrounding Richard's birthplace highlights the region's artificiality and superabundance. It creates a stark contrast to the Rubios' migrant, liminal existence:

> The Rubio family lived in a white clapboard house on a melon farm, on land that had been near desert not too long ago. On one side of the habitation ran the creek, which was lined by drab mesquites and an occasional *sausal*. To the other side, as far as the eye could see and beyond, could be seen rows and rows of melons. Here and there a clump of trees shimmered, hull-down, seemingly dancing when viewed across acres of heat. The land had been reclaimed and the valley made artificially green and fertile, but the oppressive heat remained, and the people who tilled the fields,

> for the most part, came from the temperate climate of the central plateaus of Mexico and found it difficult to acclimatize. (28–29)

Signs of acculturation and progress—the white clapboard house, the acres of greenery—are tempered by the desert's oppressive heat and the immigrants' discomfort. For them, the valley's promise is a mirage. Even though the farms grow millions of melons, the workers themselves enjoy little of the harvest.

Their brutal struggle against the desert elements is truly life or death:

> Every day, one or two or three of them were carried, dehydrated and comatose, from the field... there were a few a year who died before they could receive help, and were carted off to El Centro, where they ended up in a pauper's grave or on a slab in some medical school. (29)

Mexican migrants like the Rubios are "scattered throughout the valley," so that "it was a hardship to visit each other." Culturally marginalized, they are forced to socialize, to celebrate and mourn in private, secret, and almost invisible ways. When Juan Rubio buries Richard's afterbirth deep in the desert floor so that animals won't get at it, he performs one such secret rite, affirming the traditional cultural practices of his Mexican homeland. Burying the placenta in the earth where a child is born guarantees that he or she will always have a place to call home.

Richard Rubio, however, is not destined to stay in the Imperial Valley. Along with thousands of other immigrants from Mexico, his family takes up the perigrenaje. Pursuing seasonal work meant leading a frenetic and nomadic existence: "Lettuce harvests in Salinas, melons in Brawley, grapes in Parlier, oranges in Ontario, cotton in Firebaugh—and, finally, Santa Clara, the prune country" (31). The Rubio family's lives become molded to the migratory rhythms of modern agricultural production.

Like earlier Japanese immigrants, these first-generation Mexican Americans long to go home. With each passing year, Richard's father feels the chains of wage labor and migrancy grow "incrementally heavier on his heart." But he sets his feelings aside to give his children a shot at the American dream. Juan Rubio settles in Santa Clara, California, and urges his son to attend school and make a place for himself in this alien American world. The rest of the novel describes Richard's quest for the meaning of life in 1940s California. Like other second-generation Mexican Americans, Richard's sense of self is torn between his parents' adherence to tradition and his growing awareness of the new cultural possibilities presented by a modernizing America.

Throughout his childhood, Richard's parents treat him as though they were all still in Mexico, expecting him to adhere to traditional beliefs about race and sexuality. Invoking a long-standing Mexican conception of racial mixing (*mestizaje*), his mother says of Richard, "All indio, this boy of mine ... except inside. The Spanish blood is deep within him" (35). In Santa Clara, Juan Rubio attempts to recreate village life inside his rented, fenced-in lot. It was his own "small piece of Mexico," where "children were born, people were married, and sometimes someone, usually a newborn baby, died" (43). During the socially tumultuous thirties, Richard witnesses strikers being attacked by goons and one of his own people committing murder. It is at this juncture that Juan Rubio explains the true nature of America to his son: "All the people who are pushed around in the rest of the world come here, because they can maybe push someone else around. . . . That is why they teach their children to call you a cholo and a dirty Mexican" (100).

As he enters his teenage years, however, Richard drifts farther and farther away from his father's longing for Mexico and his mother's faith in the Christian God. The remainder of his story recounts his efforts to find something to replace the attenuated verities of his parents' worldview. He responds to this challenge by adopting a hybrid cultural identity, not quite Mexican, and not quite American. Richard announces to his Mexican girlfriend that he is "a Pocho." It is a word that Mexican nationals use as a pejorative; Richard now adopts it with pride. "We make Castilian words out of English words" (165), Richard tells his girlfriend, signaling that he had come to regard his cultural "deficiency" as a source of creativity. Coming together as group of hybrid cultural outsiders, Richard and his friends call themselves Pachucos. They speak in Pochismos, listen to Norteña music, zoop up cars, go to sock hops.

In order to make his new cultural identity more concrete, Richard turns to storytelling. "I'm gonna write books," he tells his family. Protected by the Pachuco's emerging, creative subculture, Richard attempts to realize his dream of becoming a storyteller by taking night classes in creative writing at a local school. But he is soon repelled by the reverse racism of his liberal classmates and teachers. "It bothered him," the narrator tells us, "that they should always try to find things in his life that could make him a martyr, a representative of 'his people'" (175).

Disillusioned with American society's attempt to marginalize and label him, Richard joins the navy and ships out for the war in the Pacific. Turning his back on tradition, but uncertain of where his new pocho storytelling calling will take him, he stands suspended in the moment, without a firm sense of who he really is:

> His father had won his battle, and for him life was worthwhile, but [Richard] had never been aware of what his fight was. What about me? thought Richard. Because he did not know, he would strive to live. He thought of this... and suddenly he knew that for him there would never be a coming back. (187)

Poised on the verge of becoming a writer, not quite Mexican, not quite American, Richard's betwixt and between position epitomizes both the central theme of and the point of view shared by an emerging group of storytellers about Mexican American identity that grew out of many immigrants' experiences in the Imperial Valley.

Villarreal's own biography suggests that the author was himself in search of a homeland. After a stint in the navy, Villarreal earned a degree at Berkeley in 1950 and moved around from Texas to California to Mexico before finally settling in Mexico and living out the 1970s there. Through his own travels, Villarreal seems to have come to understand that migrancy does not necessarily mean rootlessness. Perhaps he called his novel *Pocho* to point out this difference. While Richard Rubio struggles almost equally against Anglos and Mexicans, the Spanish word pocho underscores the essential Mexicanness of Richard's ordeal. "Pocho" is indeed a word for a hybrid identity. But it is important to remember that it articulates that sense of identity with *Mexicanidad* as its center. The word itself means nothing to the Anglos in Richard's world. They use terms like *greaser* and *chili bean*. For the emergent Chicano/a community to which Richard belongs, however, pocho signifies a life forever suspended between two languages and two homelands. It is a word that embodies both genius and locus, spirit and place.

During the 1960s, when Villarreal's novel was rediscovered and promoted by Chicano/a activists as an integral part of their cultural *movimiento*, Mexican American intellectuals in the West spent a great deal of time and energy pondering the meaning and nature of place for their community. In 1969, one important group decided their mythic homeland—a theoretical construct—should have a name, and christened it Aztlán. Two members of that group, Rudolfo Anaya and Francisco Lomelí, explain how the word they coined embodies two important early conceptualizations of Mexican American identity: "First, it represents the geographic region known as

Travesías

the southwestern part of the United States, composed of the territory that Mexico ceded in 1848 . . . ; second, and more important, Aztlán symbolizes the spiritual union of the Chicanos, something that is carried with the heart, no matter where they may live or where they may find themselves" (Anaya and Lomelí 8). In the late sixties, the authors recall, "Chicanos freely engaged in this necessary archaeological fabulation." Aztlán existed as "a spiritual reality," and it was "their duty to establish it as a political-territorial entity" (15).

And so it was that César Chávez and his fellow UFW marchers returned to this landscape in 1969 when the UFW organized a march through the Coachella and Imperial valleys to protest the use of illegal immigrants as strikebreakers. "It was their duty" to establish the Imperial Valley as "a political-territorial entity." To do so was central to their struggle as an emerging community. To Mexican Americans like Chávez, the Imperial Valley was at the epicenter of a story about *being* Mexican American that embraced movement and migration as essential components of identity.

It is a storytelling tradition that continues to this day. Victor Villaseñor's epic novel *Rain of Gold* (1991) also employs the Imperial Valley as a central symbol of Mexican Americans' landed, yet migratory selves. Like Villarreal, Villaseñor exploits the valley's environmental and political ironies to establish an image of Mexican American identity that is based in migrancy, yet nonetheless vibrant, productive, and real. In the novel, after surviving a perigrenaje that is both physically and psychologically harrowing, Lupe, the matriarch of a Mexican American clan, gazes out across the Lower Colorado Desert: "The Imperial Valley lay hot and flat and wide behind them, stretching grey and white for hundreds of miles. The farming communities of Brawley and Westmoreland sat like little green-checkered islands in the white-flatness of the infinite desert" (342). It is significant that Lupe perceives the desert as a "white-flatness." The word Aztlán refers to the Aztec homeland, a place of "whiteness" where tradition teaches that the ancient Mexicans were guided by their spiritual visions. In *Rain of Gold*, the Imperial Valley figures the legendary homeland as a spiritually demanding landscape, where the sands "reflected the burning sun, the right eye of God." In this image, the valley conflates the Aztec ruler of the heavens and the Christian deity in a way that echoes Villarreal's use of the valley as a figure for being pocho. It is a betwixt and between place that serves well as a homeland for a profoundly ambivalent sense of self and community.

In 1998, Simón Silva, a noted artist who was born in Mexicali and grew up in the Imperial Valley, published *Small-Town Browny*, a memoir of his life as a valley *campesino*. Like the fictional works of Villarreal and Villaseñor, Silva's nonfiction storytelling is deeply rooted in the valley's landscape and labor. The collection's subtitle—"cosecha de la vida" ("a life's harvest")—suggests it is a collation of memories "harvested" from a life of harvests. Dedicated to "anyone that has ever felt alone, frustrated, unimportant, insignificant, or invisible," the stories in *Small-Town Browny* trace the emergence of Silva's powerful imagination from the time he was twelve until he was old enough to attend college. The creativity that nurtured his later artistic achievement was born of "trying to cope with the insanity that surrounded our daily lives" (37).

The anecdotes that make up *Small Town Browny* are more akin to *cuentos* ("tales") than short stories found in cosmopolitan publications like *The New Yorker* and *Atlantic Monthly*. They partake of a Mexican literary tradition of oral tales recited in pulpits and plazas across the old Southwest to explore a moral lesson or to expose a potent irony in everyday life. Many of Silva's literary sketches gain their illustrative power from the poignant counterpoint they present to the traditional life stages of middle-class Anglo kids. When classes let out for summer, Silva's family headed up north to work in the fruit orchards. While other kids took summer vacations, Silva's dad took him to cockfights. When September rolled around, and schoolteachers inevitably asked their students what they did for summer vacation, the young Silva pondered "whether or not to tell the truth." To him, "summer vacation was just another three months to make up the best bullshit story ever" (1).

Storytelling was the only buffer the young man had against experiences like those of the Planada labor camp, where the day of the family's arrival was spent "disinfecting our new cabin," and the hour before bed, teasing out "grimacing faces" from the yellowed stains on the cabin's lumpy mattresses. When, as was often the case, a week on these mattresses left the kids infested with lice, there was ample time again for more stories about how funny his sister looked hopping around while her mother sprayed her head with Raid. When it came time to graduate from high school, Silva's story again diverged sharply from those of other valley kids. Instead of a car or a trip to Europe, he received a one-way ticket on the "Brown Bomber Express" to work in the strawberries in Washington state, rumbling up north in an old Suburban packed with "pet store rabbits in a cage, fishing rods, secondhand clothes, multicolored blankets" (90).

Silva's imagination gains texture as he becomes a young adult, and the sections of the book that deal with this period of his life employ the cuento tradition to flesh out the lives of otherwise "invisible" valley residents. In

"Ode to a Cholo," Silva recalls high school classmates labeled "'troublemakers,' 'nonachievers'"(39). In a neighborhood peopled by young men with nicknames like El Bigface Carotas and El Tweety, one named El Gato stands out in Silva's mind. He was, Silva recalls, one of those Mexican American "types"—invisible to outsiders—who give the community its backbone, its *orgullo* ("pride"). Like Richard Rubio's Pachuco friends, El Gato is a cultural hero, "a vigilante of sorts, always looking out for his raza . . . clearing a path for those of us who had been told that we had a chance at making it in life. He was always ready to make a hit on the person who was trying to put the few of us down, sacrificing himself and giving us the peace of mind that someone was watching over us" (42).

Silva's stories immerse his readers in the wash of feelings, sights, and sounds that make up the world of the Imperial Valley's workers—a world rarely experienced by outsiders. Rising every morning at 4:00 a.m. during the cotton thinning season, Silva and his neighbors board the Alfredo Flores bus for a field on the south shore of the Salton Sea. On the long ride, Silva's ears pick up the cadences of campesino life: "I heard the chisme on herbal cures, upcoming concerts, championship wrestling, and secrets about people in the neighborhood" (55). When they arrive at the field, they stumble out of the bus "like a group of Christians led to the Colosseum," and are handed "a couple of salt tablets and long-neck hoes."

At the end of his collection, Silva sums up the role of Latino storytelling in the Imperial Valley: "Most of us will not be remembered because, from a historical point of view, our lives are insignificant and invisible. If we're lucky, we'll end up a statistic worthy of news commentary. For example: Who exactly were the twelve undocumented workers who crashed off the 15 freeway last summer? Who was the woman who lost her life crossing the border yesterday? Who was the latest field worker to die of cancer?" (79). Silva's own stories shake off this anonymity to take their place among other valley storytelling traditions.

But in the Imperial Valley, a place of doubling identities and multiple perspectives, tales like those of Simón Silva are only half the story. Mexican nationals, often driven by forces of social dislocation and economic opportunity like those in the United States, also look to the land on the Mexican side of the frontier—the Mexicali Valley—in their quest to build a new postwar sense of identity. Thus, the cultural forces shaping storytelling on the northern frontier are repeated and mirrored in the stories Mexican nationals tell each other about the land that one Mexican anthropologist famously referred to as "el otro Mexico."

Ecologically and geographically, the Mexicali Valley is a continuation of the Lower Colorado. It is separated from its Anglo counterpart primarily by the politics of an international border and a distinct national history. Situated at the top of the arc of land created by the Sea of Cortez, bounded on the east by the Colorado River Delta and the west by the Pacific ocean, the Mexicali Valley anchors one of the longest peninsulas in the world to mainland Mexico and California. The peninsula is so massive that European explorers at first thought California was an island. Like its American neighbor, the Mexicali Valley is arid to the point of hardship and was offputting to humans over the many centuries that preceded its irrigation. Part of the Mexican State of Baja California, it was one of the last frontiers for population expansion and economic development after the revolution. Mexican intellectuals now call the region the *bajalta*, a term that like pocho signals its suspension between worlds and cultures. It has always been a contested zone, for both Mexicans and Americans. In 1853, for example, the American entrepreneur William Walker invaded Baja and attempted to set up a separate republic along the lines of Texas.

At the onset of the twentieth century, Baja's inland valley initially seemed destined to fall to more covert American development schemes. Its present-day capital, Mexicali, a metropolis of more than 750,000 people, began the twentieth century as a Mexican extension of the Imperial Valley town of Calexico. The two cities "were designed basically as a single urban system, in which the north-south grids of both town plans were integrated in a perfect alignment" (Lucero 94). Charles Rockwood himself drafted the first town plan. Until 1936, a full 90 percent of the agricultural land in the Mexicali Valley was owned by the Colorado River Land Company (CRLC), the investment group that developed the Imperial Valley. When the Colorado flooded in 1905-6 almost half of Mexicali was destroyed.

Because of its remoteness and sparse population, the region was little affected by the Mexican Revolution (1910-20). For most of the teens and twenties, Baja enjoyed a kind of economic prosperity and cultural insularity under the rule of Esteban Cantu, a loyalist to the overthrown dictator Porfirio Díaz. "Cantu," one historian notes, "was able to maintain a government free from the vicious revolutionary struggle that was taking place in every corner of the nation" (Lucero 97).

The Volstead Act of 1920, which outlawed the consumption of alcohol in the United States, proved an economic boon for Baja. The region soon hosted one of the most notorious casinos of the era, the Agua Caliente club of Tijuana. Hollywood stars were wont to frequent the cantinas and clubs like the Owl Café in Mexicali, seeking exotic adventures (see figure 25). Crossing the border offered Americans a heady mix of invisibility and invincibility, and they caroused publicly there in ways not possible even in Los Angeles. Mexicali was awash in booze and up all night. The Baja nightlife also established a uniquely multicultural and "modern" dynamic on the border that continues to this day. As Mexican anthropologist Fernando Jordan observed, "The dry state of the United States created a veritable Sodom and Gomorra out of the border. The North Americans were the clients, the Chinese were the money men, and the Mexicans the organizers" (Jordán 100).

In the thirties, Mexicali's economy began recovering its agricultural base, but a labor shortage—caused by the out-migration of Chinese workers during the Depression—threatened to nip the recovery in the bud. The government of Mexican president Lázaro Cardenas responded with socialist and nationalistic zeal, setting a twenty-year deadline for the CRLC's return of its properties to Mexican nationals (Lucero 104). Cardenas also implemented the *ejido* concept of communal farming on the lands being repatriated by the CRLC. Although the ejido was as old as Spanish colonization, Cardenas modernized the system so that land could be redistributed to formerly landless laborers from haciendas in other parts of Mexico. Many of the new ejido*s* were cooperatives, in which the small farmers who worked the land also owned the means of production—the irrigation canals, packing houses, and farm equipment needed to make modern agriculture a success in the reclaimed desert.

By 1946, forty-four ejidos had been established in the Mexicali Valley. The promise of land ownership and water rights, coupled with the attraction of the U.S. Bracero Program—a guest worker program in place from 1941 to 1962—created a huge influx of people into the previously sparsely populated region. By 1950, the Mexicali Valley had become Mexico's third-largest cotton-producing district. The population of Mexicali had grown to 130,000; 63 percent of its residents had been born outside the state of Baja. It would soon be Mexico's third-largest border city.

As in the Imperial Valley, Mexicali's mix of human migration, arid climate, and agricultural prosperity would inspire generations of storytellers. The cultural history of the Imperial Valley's Mexican twin, however, would cause its stories to diverge from the tales of isolation and progress spun by its American neighbor. Mexicali writers turned instead to urban tales of greed and corruption, collectivity, and cosmopolitanism. For local cultural critic and crime novelist Gabriel Trujillo Muñoz, the story of Mexicali's cultural development is not a tale of humans battling an alien desert, but rather of a cosmopolitan metropolis founded on a geopolitical frontier. Its urban infrastructure—the streets, cantinas, theaters, and parks—become the crucible within which diverse peoples from around Mexico collaborate, debate, and struggle to produce "la cultura bajacaliforniense." The looming presence of the United States gives their cultural performances an edge that other parts of Mexico cannot duplicate. In Mexicali, Trujillo believes, a special cultural formation has been born. He calls it an "aglomeración" (a teeming mix), an "encrucijada" (a crossroads quandry)—fitting descriptions of an emerging cosmopolitan consciousness that is at once rooted in an agricultural economy, a desert landscape, and an international border crossing.

Mexicali's birth as a *bajalta* storytelling cosmopolis began inauspiciously enough. In 1910 when the city was founded, Baja California, like the rest of Mexico, was deeply engaged in celebrating Mexican independence. Music, pageants, and other forms of political propaganda exhalted the autocratic rule of Porifirio Díaz. For Mexicali's middle class, Trujillo observes, "rebellious social culture or revolutionary struggle" held little appeal (Trujillo, *Mexicali* 18). Cultural activities were mostly "a pretext for the comfortable search for an untroubled future" (Trujillo, *Mexicali* 16). The city's cultural life was dominated by the landed gentry, whose cultural attachments were closer to the United States and Europe than to Latin America. In the Parque Niños Heroes, built along the international border, Mexican musicians performed a classical repertoire for listeners seated on both sides of the boundary line.

It was not until the twenties that revolutionary artists from the south moved into the region and embarked on the kind of socially engaged work that had already been going on in Mexico City for a decade. As the border city began to experience the broader "vida communitaria" promulgated by revolutionaries in the rest of the country, the virtually forgotten province launched a campaign to reintroduce itself to the rest of Mexico. With the arrival of brothers Facundo and Francisco Bernal in 1920, Mexicali literature moved for the first time into a revolutionary mode. The Bernals produced world-weary, somewhat pessimistic verse that was a stark contrast to the self-satisfied productions of Mexicali artists during the Cantu era. The brothers spoke for "the disenfranchised" and against "hypocritical conventionalism" (Trujillo, *Mexicali* 20).

Revolutionary arts in Mexicali were, however, always tempered by the city's border location. Its proximity to America and its population's intimate connections with the great water project to the north represented forces too great to ignore. In 1936, the Colorado River Land Company commissioned bucolic murals for its Mexicali office that featured a Mexican woman balancing water on her head in the traditional village way. Clearly, the Mexicali

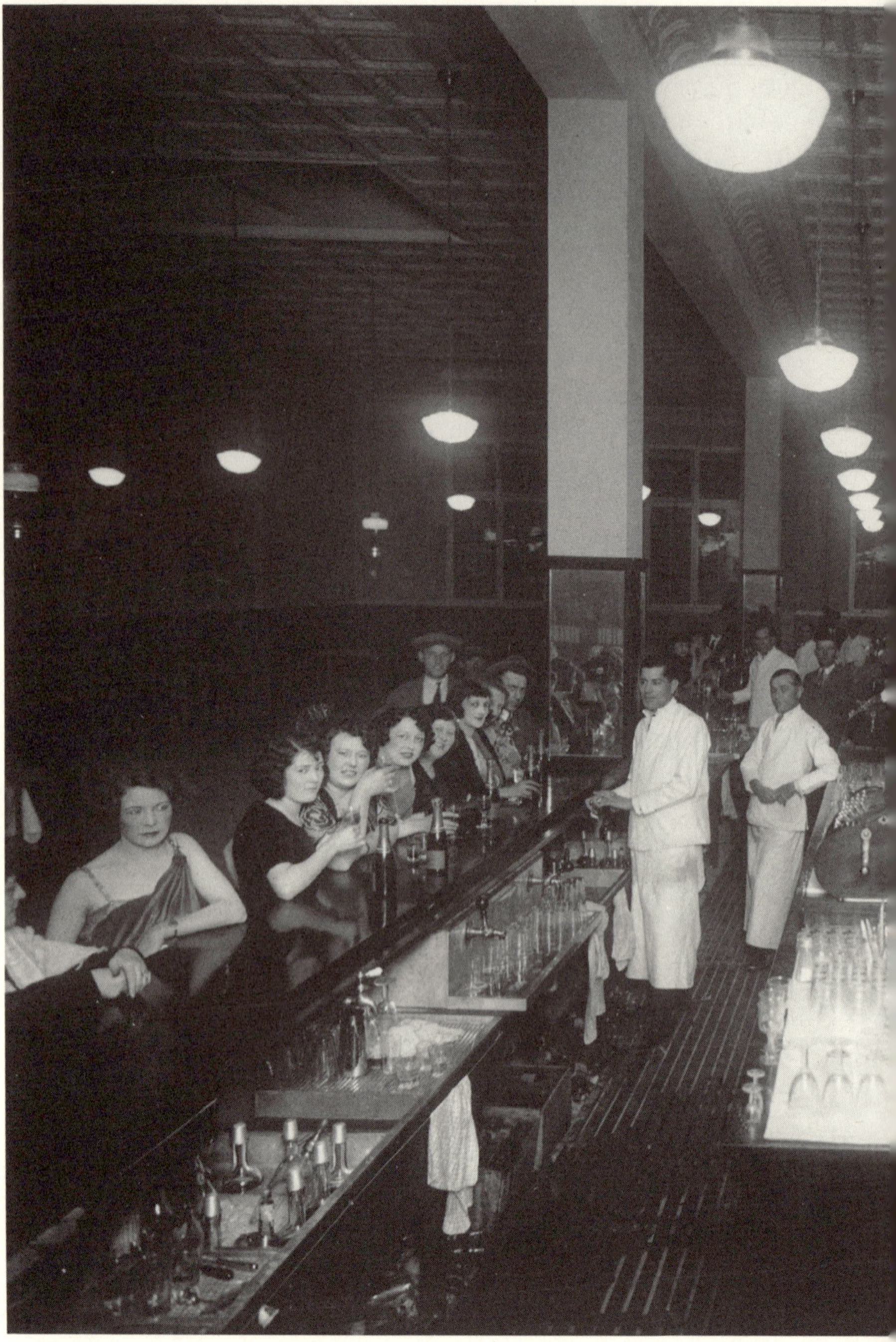

FIGURE 25.
Leo Hetzel, *The Owl Café, Mexicali.* Imperial County Historical Society.

| 143

elites were invoking a pastoral vision of progress similar to that immortalized on the walls of the Imperial Valley's Barbara Worth Hotel. Mexicali artists also celebrated the "divine kiss of water and sun" that was the region's own progressive miracle. Trujillo describes the Mexicali cultural horizon of the 1930s and 1940s as "a space dominated by absolute confidence in modernity and progress" (*Mexicali* 32).

Over the next thirty years, however, Baja California stories about land and water would diverge significantly from those of the Imperial Valley. Immigrants to Mexicali brought with them a "heterogeneous cultural baggage, drawn from every region of the country" (Trujillo, *Mexicali* 34). Much more than the triumph of humans over the desert, it was the collision of these various village traditions with the staid, bourgeois cultural infrastructure of the border city that energized Mexicali's final cultural coming of age. By the 1950s, the Mexican anthropologist Fernando Jordán would call the region an *otro* Mexico. Unlike the Imperial Valley, where cultural producers often worked to insulate the valley from change, Mexicali artists began to exploit the acknowledged cultural tensions of the city—tensions between the urban and rural, Baja and the rest of the nation, the United States and Mexico.

The fictional works of Gabriel Trujillo Muñoz explore this Mexican struggle with the meaning of Baja and its sister border regions in the national consciousness. Like Villarreal, Villaseñor, and Silva, Trujillo draws on autobiographical insights and local knowledge to forge a postmodern Mexican identity that realizes those "distinctive voices, at times complementary, at times contrapuntal" that have gone into the making of this place (*Mexicali* 10). Trujillo's *narcotraffico* border saga, *El Festín de los Cuervos* (The Feast of the Crows, 2002), is his most recent and incisive fictional account of present-day "Mexicalienses" consciousness. It thus represents the cutting edge in Lower Colorado storytelling from the Mexican perspective. A five-novella collection of detective fiction, *El Festín de los Cuervos* features the cases of Miguel Angel Morgado, a grey-eyed Mexicali-born lawyer who has spent most of his career working on human rights law in Mexico City, but who finds himself drawn increasingly into criminal investigations. In many ways, Morgado is Trujillo's alter ego, for the detective novelist was himself born and raised in Mexicali, educated in Mexico City, where he earned a medical degree, only to return to his hometown later in life to occupy the cultural position of a sort of writer-in-residence for the border metropolis.

The first novella in the collection is *Mesquite Road*, a story in which Morgado is called back to Mexicali to solve the murder of an old family friend. It opens with a vicious parody of regionalist landscape description. As the narrator describes a pastoral desert scene with the sun rising on the Lower Colorado like an image from a Hallmark card, he glances over the small clot of flies hovering around some burlap bags lying innocently in the foreground. As the sun breaks over the mountains, its rays illuminate the grisly truth briefly obscured by the desert's predawn beauty—the bags contain the battered, dismembered bodies of nameless murder victims.

Meanwhile, in the Mexico City airport, Morgado is waiting for a plane to Mexicali. In an exchange with another passenger, he tries to explain what and where Mexicali is:

> Mexicali?—asked the president of the Guanajuato Bar Association.
> Isn't that in the States?
> No!—responded Morgado, irritated—the border, it's in Baja California.
> Yeah, man, interrupted Ochoa—, they've got *maquiladoras*, fine
>   babes ... A normal community, like the Adams family.
> It's an agricultural and industrial region, Morgado tried to explain.
> Sounds boring, brother. Me, I prefer Tijuana. Better than Tijuana,
>   San Diego.
>   (Trujillo, *Festín* 17)

This opening dialog sets up the novella's main theme of a modern, alienated Mexican intellectual attempting to come to terms with his local history. In it, he attempts to locate his genius and locus, at a time when Mexico and Mexicans are becoming increasingly implicated in a global economy and transnational identities.

Trujillo's story about the Imperial and Mexicali valleys engages his fictionalized personal reminiscences about growing up in Mexicali to explore the larger question of what it means to be Mexican at the end of the twentieth century. After the exchange about Mexicali at the airport, Morgado grows pensive:

> The conversation had provoked conflicting feelings. The subject of
> Mexicali produced, automatically, certain images: his infancy, the
> loss of his mother, the madness of his father, the border and its barbed
> wire. And with them rose the detachment, the forgotten bonds, the
> alienation. His life did not revolve around that distant northern
> land, that desert, that fiery horizon. But the connections were not
> completely broken ... old feelings quickly resurfaced whenever he
> returned to the city where he was born. (Trujillo, *Festín* 17-18)

Like other people of this valley, Morgado finds that even though his life is no longer *in* the borderlands, the borderlands somehow remain in *him*.

Morgado arrives in a city that is both like and unlike the one he left as a youth. "The same sun, the same climate" assaults him as he disembarks at the Mexicali airport. When he asks a friend whether "the gringos are still friendly," however, the answer is jarring. "No, those days are gone," Atanasio tells him. It is Atanasio who has called Morgado back home to solve a killing that local officials have chalked up to narcotrafficking.

To sort out the crime, Morgado must face his own demons. He must also, Atanasio warns him, "Ease up on the nostalgia and take the city as it is now. Not the way it once was." Atanasio points out that the "heart of Mexicali" is now "a place of solace for the disenfranchised, the deracinated and the valiant" (Trujillo, *Festín* 111). He has Morgado close his eyes and listen to the sounds of the city, to the accordion of Ramón Ayala, Norteñas, English language rock and roll, cumbias, and boleros.

While the old friends catch up, we learn that Atanasio is still committed to anarchy as a political philosophy. He feels that anarchism is a perfectly rational response to an ineffectual Mexican political system where the PRI (Partido Revolucionario Institucional) gives way to PAN (Partido Acción Nacional) and PAN to PRI and nothing ever changes. Morgado agrees with the diagnosis, but not the cure. His own politics consist of a somewhat wistful and cosmopolitan blend of Marxism and liberation theology.

As Morgado unravels the murder, however, he moves closer to self-discovery and a rejection of those politics. Solving *this* crime will depend on his ability to disentangle the border city from the nostalgic memories of his youth and from his country's stereotyped oversimplifications of the region. Morgado's new Mexicali, the one he "discovers" on his way to solving the murder, is postmodern. It exists in the Mexico of Vicente Fox, the first president to be elected from a party other than the entrenched and corrupt PRI. This is a Mexico of ever more ironic contrasts, as promises of new beginnings and optimistic futures give way to "the same old thing."

The case takes Morgado from the stark, sun-flooded streets of Mexicali to the sleazy bars of its red-light district. It is a vertiginous journey between light and dark that mocks his cosmopolitan faith in easy distinctions between right and wrong. By day, the brilliant desert sun obscures as much as it reveals, and the desert's heat seems to bring down "the weight of the world on your shoulders" (Trujillo, *Festín* 60). Ironically, everyone *except* the politicians wear Ray Bans to protect their eyes from the glare.

By night the heat remains, but neon and darkening shadows transform the city into a vision of the underworld. The clues lead to Commandante Zamudio, chief of the judicial police, whose ranch, Los Mesquites, gives the story its name. But just when the tale is beginning to sound like the same old story of prerevolutionary corruption in Mexico, the perspective shifts. In other nightspots, Morgado finds a new Mexico, one deeply intertwined with American popular culture and wrapped up in complex, postmodern plots and motivations that spring from the geopolitics of the region.

As he sifts for clues in these two Mexicos—one postmodern, the other prerevolutionary—Morgado finds himself increasingly drawn back into his own conflicted past. He reunites briefly with his senile father, and the meeting gives Trujillo another opportunity to explore a side of Mexico that is trapped in the past. All that is left to Morgado's father are memories of the good old days when he was a violinist among the Cantu bourgeoisie. Other Mexicali residents of his father's generation agree that the city is falling apart but lay the blame on Mexican outsiders who have come from other provinces. Morgado hears a long-time resident exclaim, "Those Qaxaquins, they only come to dirty up our streets" (Trujillo, *Festín* 72). This "purist" local vision cannot hope to offer cultural or political solace to a modern, globalizing Mexico, and throughout the book Trujillo satirizes the nostalgic regionalism that fosters this point of view.

With contemporary Mexicali increasingly challenging his faith—in justice, in the nostalgic borderlands of his youth—Morgado turns to rationality and facts as a way out. He smells a conspiracy and decides to cross the border to get the American side of the story. But American facts prove just as tenuous as Mexican fabulation. Morgado is roughed up at the border by a Chicano INS agent, then witnesses a group of illegals scattering across the highway north of Calexico and losing themselves in the valley's fields. When he tunes in his car radio, he hears a bicultural, bilingual announcement of cross-border *Mexicanidad*: "This is for all our listeners in Mexicali and our neighbor Imperial Valley, for all Mexicans, wet or dry" (Trujillo, *Festín* 80).

Harry Davalos, a DEA agent Morgado meets in El Centro, offers little solace. The border of Mexicali today, Davalos informs him, is in the middle of "an undeclared war, like in Nicaragua" (81). It's all about greed, the Good Neighbor Policy, distrust, and suspicion. Fueled by North America's thirst for contraband, the border is host to the drug war's violent repercussions. At the epicenter of this particular round of that war, Davalos tells Morgado, is a little rancho called Los Mezquites, where the murder victim has been foreman.

The story ends as it begins, in a maelstrom of violence and death. At the hacienda Los Mesquites, a symbol of old patriarchal Mexico, a huge gun battle ensues. By the end of the day, all the principal suspects have been gunned down by assailants known and unknown. Yet the original murder remains as mysterious as when Morgado began the investigation. On the return trip to Mexicali across a stretch of desert, he hears a radio evangelist predict the end of the world, while outside his car, it is "a typical border night, with a full moon and howling coyotes" (104). The jarring juxtaposition of regionalist nostalgia and postmodern apocalypse yield one message: you can't go home again.

Morgado once again ponders the meaning of self and homeland, this time with a new perspective:

> Life in Mexicali—and not because of the extreme heat—was precarious and fleeting. An electric spark. You marked time here in a different way, with a greater intensity. This is a city that had traveled in one century the distance that it took other cities a thousand years to traverse. (Trujillo, *Festín* 123-24)

Standing amid a sea of humanity on a busy Mexicali street, Morgado finally feels membership in the postmodern "multitude"—"Yankee tourists, . . . taco venders and whores, impotent cops and blind beggars, impassive chinamen, and preachers of the second coming . . . fermenting in the same cultural soup" (124).

Yet nagging questions remain. Packing for his return trip to Mexico City, Morgado is interrupted a final time by DEA agent Harry Davalos, whom he presses for answers:

> There are more things behind this, right? . . . When are you going to leave us alone?
> Who?
> You, gringos, us Mexicans.
> Never, We're neighbors. Or did you forget?
>
> (Trujillo, *Festín* 129)

On the plane, Morgado opens Atanasio's parting gift, the novel *The Lawless Roads* (1939) by Graham Greene. The British writer's words sting him with a revelatory force: "The border means more than a customs house, a passport officer, a man with a gun. Over there, everything is going to be different" (142). The novel's last words are also Greene's: "When people die on the border, they call it 'a happy death'" (143).

"Happy"—according to Greene—because they are gazing hopefully to the other side, to the next moment. But for Morgado, it is an ironic happiness. He has faced himself down in the border town of his youth only to lose himself again in the border's infinite regress. Morgado's irony is, by extension, Mexico's own. Closing with a British colonial writer's perspective is fitting tribute to Trujillo's sense that contemporary Mexican identity, especially in places like Mexicali, is a complex blend of colonialism and localism, the national and transnational, the personal and collective.

For Mexican storytellers, both native and American born, the Mexicali and Imperial valleys offer geopolitical spaces from which to meditate on the border's many mirrors. Beneath its sun-baked surface, the Lower Colorado is a profoundly modern place. Stories emerge there of human selves divided by cultures, politics, and geography. For storytellers sensitive to this modernity, it is impossible to separate land from the human presence on the land. For them, the imaginary engineering of an international border through this contiguous Mexican homeland is far more potent and interesting than any story about reclamation or isolation or progress. Unlike the All-American canal, so indisputably present in the sand hills of the eastern Imperial Valley, the border is itself mostly absent from the scene. It is a cosmopolitan dream imposed on this landscape from far away—much like Miguel Angel Morgado's liberation politics—and like them, doomed to founder in this impossible land.

On any given day, you can drive along Interstate 8 through the valley as it shadows this imaginary line and see Border Patrol SUVs poised at regular intervals along bluffs on the American side. The drivers train huge field glasses off into an incalculable distance across a line that isn't really there. United States armed militias, called Minutemen, patrol the Imperial Valley's deserts, urging Congress and the president to go even further, to build a fifteen-foot-high wall across the desert to keep the Mexicans out. They tell a story in which they figure themselves as modern versions of the militias of the original thirteen colonies. Like the Minutemen of old, they stand guard against invaders who would enslave us. Mexican storytellers, on the other hand, offer a bridge, a *travesía*, a crossing:

> Between the two Californias
> I want to build a bridge,
> So whenever you wish
> You can cross from south to north,
> Walking freely
> Not like a wild rabbit.
> (Gina Valdés, untitled poem, *Puentes y Fronteras*)

7 A Heart of Fire

| In America, there is no land that is not Indian land, and in the Imperial Valley, stories of the Native landscape remain alive today, even though Euro American storytellers did their best to convince their readers that the Indians were long gone and their stories best forgotten.

For at least two centuries, the valley has been home to four distinct Native communities. Their stories about the Lower Colorado's landforms and how the first humans came to make it their home have become an organic part of the valley's narrative composition, responsible in some places for its very shape and color. Along the valley's northern margins, the Cahuilla relate how Mukat, one of two creator twins, was ceremonially cremated by the community and how from his ashes sprang the acorns, squash, and sage that would sustain them. Every spring, they sing Bird Songs, a complex cycle of migration stories that tell how each of the Cahuilla clans came to occupy its location within the homeland.

In the southwest corner of the valley, the Kumeyaay of northern Baja and San Diego County also trace their origins to powerful twin creators—Tucaypa and Yokomatic. They tell stories about long migrations south from Spirit Mountain, near Needles, California, to the historical village site called

Indian Wells. Finally, south and east along the flood plain of the Colorado, are the Quechan and the Cocopa—Yuman-speaking peoples whose language and traditions connect them to this desert landscape in a shared creation story. Like the Kumeyaay, they come from Avikame, Spirit Mountain. They too moved south, and their stories tell how the spirit of their culture hero, Marxókuvék, inhabits the rocky summit of a mountain just southwest of Yuma. According to the stories, when Marxókuvék died, the Quechan, like the Cahuilla, cremated him according to his sacred wishes. When Coyote dragged his heart from the ashes of the funeral pyre, the blood that dripped from it transformed the earth. Where each drop fell the land received a new name. Here, Greasy Mountain, there Red Dirt, and further on, Black Earth.

Such stories were sung and recited in the valley both before and after Europeans arrived. For the most part, the newcomers chose to ignore them, spinning tales of their own, transforming the desert into a blank canvas on which to perform heroic deeds of progress and civilization. Francisco Patencio, a Cahuilla elder, used to tell a story about the formation of the great Salton Basin that illuminates both Native storytelling traditions and the European practice of silencing them:

> The Indians were often asked about the dark lines against the mountainsides, down in the Coachella Valley. Many times in the early days this question was asked. When the Indians answered, "The ocean, [had made them]" they were laughed at. So the Indians did not speak much. (Patencio 103)

Records dating back as far as the eighteenth century document European disbelief of Native desert tales. Father Garces, a member of the Anza expedition, remarked in his diary, "As we were always hearing all sorts of stories from the Indians, we did not at the time give much weight to the news" (Patencio 101).

John C. Van Dyke silenced Indian storytelling to make room for his aesthetic flights of fancy in the Big Bowl. To prove that his own appreciation of this landscape was special, he first had to demonstrate that its Native peoples were unable to appreciate it at all. Robert H. Forbes, a scientist from Arizona, called Van Dyke on his glaring omission of Indian lore. Van Dyke had claimed that "the Indians have no tradition" about how the Salton Basin was formed (45). Forbes was quick to point out that there was well-known Cocopa story about the sea's comings and goings in the valley. Van Dyke's version of the tale trivialized Native storytelling:

Tradition told that the Evil Spirit dwelt there, and it was his hot breath that came up every morning on the wind, scorching and burning the brown faces of the mountain-dwellers! Fire—he dwelt in fire. Whence came all the fierce glow of sunset down over that desert if it was not the reflection from his dwelling place?.... It was a land of fire. No food, no grass, no water.... How often the tribe had lost from its numbers—slain by the heat and drought in that waste! More than once the bodies had been found by crossing bands and always the same tale was told. (15)

Contrast Van Dyke's myth with Francisco Patencio's recollection of one traditional story about the desert: "The land is close to the people because, as old man Pedro Chino used to say, 'This land is alive. It is alive.' In Cahuilla, what he was saying to me is that the heart is fire, the heart of the land. He said, 'that is why you can see where it breathes. Like in Montana where the steam comes out.' 'If it doesn't,' he said, 'it will blow up. It had to breathe, the earth'" (Patencio 56).

Neither a malevolent deity nor an unfathomable silence, the Salton Trough in the Cahuilla storytelling tradition is a living, breathing being with a heart of fire. Yet between heartbeats and the gathering of breath, this land rests in silence. And it is the natural silence of this below sea-level arid basin that provides a foundation for Native stories of this place. Here, as in many American Indian traditions, silence lies at the heart of storytelling. N. Scott Momaday, in fact, reminds us that in the Indian world, "a word is spoken or sung not against, but within the silence." In this valley, it is the silence peculiar to precisely these landforms—their geologic and human histories—that grounds the stories of the Cahuilla, Kumeyaay, Quechan, and Cocopa. Like light, sound travels differently down here. "The Eye of the Flute," written by Chumash/O'Odham poet Georgiana Valoyce-Sanchez, describes the power of this stillness from a Native perspective. It is a "Silence that holds all songs / That holds the breath / To play all songs / To Life" (*Rattles and Clappers* 75–76).

I first began to listen to this element of the valley's silence a few years ago, when I chanced across a small book called *Delfina Cuero: Her Autobiography*. It caught my eye because the cover featured a black and white photograph of a woman sitting on a large boulder with a traditional grinding stone in her hand. The desert background seemed very familiar, and when I looked over the introduction, I discovered that indeed, the photograph reproduced a horizon from the western foothills of the Imperial Valley.

Putting aside everything else, I read the sixty-three-page autobiography in one sitting. In a few hours I learned of a traditional people—the

Kumeyaay—whose homeland was the same California countryside I grew up in, yet who had remained invisible to me until this moment. In rereading Delfina Cuero's story, I became aware of an undercurrent of lament. "There is more to it," she kept saying, "but this is all I can remember." Delfina Cuero's refrain led me to wonder about the nature of Native storytelling and its place in the Lower Colorado. What was it that I knew nothing of and that she couldn't quite remember?

Delfina Cuero's story recounts her life as a member of the Kumeyaay (pronounced kum ə ya· y) people who originally inhabited a large geographic region that spread from the San Diego coastline in the west to the Colorado River in the east, in a wide band that reached from Baja to Alta California. The Kumeyaay were known in Euro American ethnographic literature up through the 1970s as the "Diegueño." They are also often called "Mission Indians" because many of their ancestors lived under the Spanish colonial mission system in the late eighteenth and early nineteenth centuries.

When Father Junipero Serra established the first California mission in 1769—the mission San Diego de Alcalá—he did so on traditional Kumeyaay lands overlooking San Diego Bay. Soon the Spanish missionaries were seizing small groups of Kumeyaay people and forcing them to work at the mission, releasing them only after they had "heard" the word of God. It is not surprising that the Kumeyaay became the most stubborn and violent opponents of Franciscan and Dominican efforts to control native California through the mission system.

By 1834, the Mexican government had secularized the California missions and turned the old religious communes into large, private haciendas. In this manifestation of colonialism, Native people like the Kumeyaay often found themselves further dispossessed of territory, living as virtual serfs in the country of their ancestors. In the 1840s, the first wave of Americans arrived, and as cities like San Diego grew on Kumeyaay lands, the American government established inland reservations for Mission Indians whose tribal communities were officially recognized as "nations." Several bands of Delfina Cuero's people, however, were left out of the reservation system. As a culture that depended on migratory patterns tied to food resources and sacred land formations, the Kumeyaay were too mobile and dispersed to fit the rigid political definitions of an Indian tribe. Many would remain unrecognized by the American government into the twentieth century.

With their traditional lands disappearing behind fences, and the path to the newly established reservations of eastern San Diego County blocked by politics, several Kumeyaay bands were compelled to live in San Diego slums, or to camp in nearby hills. As more Americans arrived to claim land and co-opt resources, many began to drift off into Mexico. By the 1890s the Kumeyaay were more or less invisible to outsiders. They were viewed not as traditional tribal people but as individual low-skilled laborers, to be hired at subsistence wages as ranch hands, miners, or domestics.

Delfina Cuero lived in the Californian/Mexican borderlands from 1900 until her death in 1972. She spent most of those years migrating on foot, following the seasonal cycle of natural food harvests. Her "autobiography," a written transcription of an oral narration made in 1967 by Florence Shipek, an anthropologist and professor of American Indian history, was initially assembled to provide evidence of Cuero's U.S. citizenship in lieu of the normal documentary proof required when she found herself on the "wrong" side of the international border during an extended period of habitation in Baja California. As she recounts the experiences of one band of Kumeyaay people in the early twentieth century, she highlights the changing role of silence and storytelling, land and culture, in a traditional society beleaguered by the economic depredations of colonialism and the cultural confusion of border politics.

Land centered the Kumeyaay's sense of who they were as a people, providing not only food and shelter, but also sacred places of worship. Because of their homeland's harsh climatic transitions, Delfina Cuero's band developed a yearly migratory cycle of hunting and gathering centered around semipermanent home camps (known as *rancherias*) in San Diego's Mission Valley. In those days, "the Indians had names for every little spot . . . each name meant something about that place" (Cuero 24). In April and May, the Kumeyaay came down to the Imperial Valley Desert foothills from the coast in search of mescal plants and to trade with their desert cousins, the Tipai, for "mesquite beans and other things from the desert" (33). In the fall, they would trek into the mountains to collect acorns. The rest of the year, they stayed closer to home near the San Diego Bay, spearing fish with cactus-thorn spears, harvesting shellfish by the shore, or gathering pine nuts in the coastal groves. Around their more permanent brush and reed dwellings in San Diego's Mission Valley, they cultivated small gardens.

Even with the influx of Europeans, the coastal Kumeyaay way of life for a time held its own. Although outsiders like Garces and Van Dyke dismissed their cultural traditions as "superstition" or "lies," the Kumeyaay's traditional ways remained highly regulated, as they had been in the "olden" days: "There were many . . . rules and things we were taught and believed. There were rules so that each one knew what to do all the time" (Cuero 47).

Men and women wore their facial tattoos proudly, for they were believed to "help you go on the straight road" (40). Cuero's husband, Sebastian Osun, had a tattoo on his forehead—"it was real pretty, blue-green and real round, like the moon and about the size of a half dollar" (39). The song cycles of the yearly fire dance (the *kuruk*) reaffirmed the vitality of Kumeyaay culture: "The songs that go with it have to be sung in the right order, from early evening until dawn. There is a song for each time of the night and as the sun is rising. It was danced at the death of a person and also to welcome a new child" (46).

However, when "white people kept moving into more and more of the places," Cuero recalls, "we couldn't camp around those places anymore. We went farther and farther from San Diego, looking for places where nobody chased us away" (26). The Kumeyaay sought refuge in the less-populated backcountry of Baja California. Cuero's grandparents "crossed the line first" without any sense of its sociopolitical meaning: "We didn't know it was a line, only that nobody chased [us] away." (26). To Delfina Cuero and her family, the frontera "was just a place in the whole area that had belonged to the Indians where nobody told us to move on" (54).

With this forced migration came cultural dislocation. The first things to go were the simple kitchen gardens of the base settlements: "We had to move too much to plant anything. Always being told to leave, it was no use to plant" (32). Next, the Kumeyaay's life-sustaining medicinal herbs became more difficult to find: "We [couldn't] go everywhere to look for them" (45). Finally, the migratory rhythms themselves ceased: "Our family went down to the beach below Ensenada and to Rosarito Beach when we couldn't get to the San Diego beaches anymore" (56).

As the travels of the Kumeyaay ranged farther and wider, clan relationships were stretched thin. Under the pressures of this enforced restlessness and the weakening of the integrated network of rules and responsibilities, Cuero's father deserted the family. To survive, her mother asked Delfina "to get married so that there would be a man to hunt for us" (54).

For a time, Delfina explains, "everything was all right." Her husband Sebastian "was a good man. He worked hard. . . . He was real good to me. He took care of the children" (55). In spite of the forces that led her father to abandon the family, Cuero's immediate group, under the leadership of Sebastian, struggled to live the traditional Kumeyaay way in a time of extreme dearth. But when Sebastian died unexpectedly, there was no longer the extended Kumeyaay clan system for Delfina Cuero to fall back on in support of her children and herself. Although she cut her hair off in "the Indian way," she soon found that a single person couldn't sustain a hunting and gathering existence: "I had a hard time getting enough food for my children. Things got pretty bad" (60). So bad, in fact, that she was forced to sacrifice her oldest son to support the others: "I finally had to sell Aureliano to a Mexican to get food" (60).

Yet Delfina Cuero's life story does not merely recount the oppression of a Native population on the border. It also demonstrates the Kumeyaay's capacity for cultural renewal through storytelling. Cuero's people may have been "exiled" from the rancherias and kitchen gardens and pushed into Mexico, but the land remained "home" because they "had names for every little place," because they had stories to prove it. Delfina Cuero's autobiography is itself one kind of modern Kumeyaay story of place, and as she recounts the events of her life to demonstrate her "citizenship," she focuses on one special ceremony that seems to represent the storytelling key to her present situation. That story is made up of the songs cycles and myths of the initiation rite of Kumeyaay girls into womanhood.

This ritual is one source of her autobiography's refrain ("there is more to it, but that is all I can remember"). She herself had missed out on the important rite because of the cultural dislocations caused by European intrusions in the region: "My grandmother told me about what they did to girls as they were about to become women. But I'm not that old! They had already stopped doing it when I became a woman" (39). From the silence of colonial repression, however, sprang a new kind of story, as Delfina Cuero describes what her grandmother told her of this ceremony of womanhood. In doing so she recovers some form of a ceremony that is perhaps the Kumeyaay's oldest and the one least changed by outside influence.

She remembers how her grandmother emphasized the ceremony's importance, many times reciting how young girls were for a short time literally interred in the earth of their homeland:

> They dug a hole, filled it with warm sand, and kept the girl in there. They tattooed her all around her mouth and chin. They would sing about food and see if she would get hungry; to see if she could stand hunger. She wasn't allowed to eat. They danced around the top of the hole. A week I think they kept her there, I'm not sure. They didn't want the girls to get wrinkled early or to get gray, but to have good health and good babies. This helped them. I believe in it, but they didn't ask me. I don't get sick much, but I am gray and wrinkled. (39)

A few pages later, Delfina Cuero outlines the very practical importance the ceremony had for a twentieth-century Kumeyaay woman. Pregnant for the first time and working miles from home on her own, Delfina was suddenly stricken with a crippling pain:

> I started walking back home but I had to stop and rest when the pain was too much. Then the baby came, I couldn't walk any more, and I didn't know what to do. Finally an uncle came out looking for me when I didn't return. My grandmother had not realized my time was so close or she would have not let me go so far alone. They carried me back but I lost the baby. (43)

The song cycle of the girl's ceremony contained important knowledge about all aspects of Kumeyaay womanhood, including information about childbirth. Without these songs, Delfina Cuero lost a baby, and it seems that her sad experience was shared by many Kumeyaay women of her generation: "Some of the other girls had the same trouble I did." (43).

But the songs and ritual served other purposes as well. In the ceremony, hunger is depicted as communal and is alleviated by "the songs and the myths that belonged to the ceremony" (42). In the old days, the songs and the myths "fed" the girl with the cultural sustenance she would need throughout her life. But in Delfina Cuero's twentieth-century borderlands' world, songs and myths are hard to come by. When, for example, she attempts to relate a story about starfish early in the narrative, she is unable to remember it, and excuses herself by saying, "There was more to it but I am not a storyteller and that is all I can remember" (29). In traditional Kumeyaay culture, there were special people with the ability to tell stories and they fulfilled that duty for their group (Cuero's grandfather was one).

In those days, "the old people did not have to tell us what the story explained at the end of the story." Now, however, Delfina must explain to her ethnographer what it all means—to prove she is who she says she is, to bring the outsider into her homeland to help her reclaim it. While explaining what the Kumeyaay women learned in the ritual songs of initiation, she remarks, "Nobody just talked about these things ever. It was all in the songs and myths that belonged to the ceremony" (42). By calling her storytelling "just talk," Cuero indicates that it represents a new and special kind of language, related to her new circumstances. And it is in this aspect of her autobiography that one may glimpse the many layers of historical interaction and colonial repression that make Delfina Cuero's life story a particularly telling example of how landscape, history, and narrative are born of the storied silence of Native life on the borderlands in the twentieth century.

First and foremost, the twentieth-century borderlands demand that Delfina Cuero perform a political identity and a political language. She must "just talk" her way back into the United States. The tales she narrates are thus full of comments that have less to do with ethnography than with her effort to convince a U.S. court of her legal right to live in her traditional homelands. Clearly recognizing the pragmatic value of her story, Cuero disrupts its flow to exhort an imagined audience of powers-that-be: "I pray that something will work out so that my children and grandchildren can come back with me to where I was born" (67). Appealing to the bottom-line mentality of such an audience, she says, "I would like to come back to where I was born for good if I could. I would do anything to work to make a living" (65).

Additionally, the borderland demands that she find new ways to reach out to her ancestors in the earth. She must engage them in a dialogue about the nature of her own identity even as she explains their world to outsiders in order to make their homeland her own again. Kumeyaay were traditionally forbidden to "just talk" to outsiders about such things. "In the course of this research," Shipek points out, Delfina Cuero was "asked to break one more custom, one which was difficult and mentally painful to break: a taboo on the discussion of, and the naming of, deceased relatives and friends" (12). When she violates this prohibition, it seems to create a chasm between her and her ancestors so that she will never be able to regain their songs and stories.

But such "talk" had already become a new kind of storytelling for the Kumeyaay in the twentieth century. This fact is beautifully illustrated in a linguist's direct transcription of a Kumeyaay man's speech made in 1954. In the 1950s, ethnographers combed Southern California for Native speakers of traditional languages in the tribal communities that were rapidly being displaced by postwar development. Some brought books with stick figures, hoping such neutral prompts would both help to prevent the intrusion of their own Euro American biases and allow Native speakers to describe everyday scenes in their own words. Responses were taped for later generations of ethnographers to use in assembling grammars of the various Southern California languages.

When Kumeyaay tribal member Ramón Ames was asked to describe what he saw in a stick-figure representation of a "single male foreground, pointing at tree, background," he responded in his Native language like this:

> As far as I can see he seems to be walking. I wonder where he's going. I don't know, but it seems to me, he's standing somewhere. Going. But as far as I can see, he seems to have no eyes. It seems to me that he has no hair. I wonder if you people know... I wonder if any of you know what he is doing. (Hayes 186)

Ramón Ames's last question is a good one, and it is this sort of reflexive response that seems to be imbedded in Delfina Cuero's "talk" as well. But perhaps even more significant is his emphasis on *going*. It reflects an important element in Native storytelling that often gets repressed by European editorial efforts to make native people's stories "less repetitive," more linear and climactic in narrative form.

His emphasis on going also reflects a deep sense of place, though it may seem rather abstract to outsiders. The linguists who interviewed him, for example, didn't quite know what to make of his response to an image of a "cow grazing in foreground, mountains in background." After Ames elucidated the scene as "a cow standing, we see him," he set off on a much longer story that begins, "long time ago this was Indian land . . ." He was promptly cut off by his transcriber. Only the linguist's gloss remains: "(10 minutes of Mission Indian history)." The dwindling land base that Delfina Cuero describes in detail finds its storytelling analog in the shrinking linguistic field allowed Native speakers by their European neighbors. Both Ramón Ames and Delfina Cuero wish to tell a larger story than the one that fits neatly into a linguist's journal or a government report.

Speech in places like the Imperial Valley has become for native speakers—in the words of Ramón Ames—"a new language we've got." That new language oscillates between "talk" and "silence," song and myth, in a distinctive cadence that echoes the region's history of colonization and dispossession.

As Mexican and Mexican American storytellers in the Mexicali and Imperial valleys have discovered, the ironic "fact" of the international border ("the line" of which Delfina's people were not even aware) is the single most important geological feature of their present-day homelands. The border is landscape, even if imposed from the outside and essentially invisible to the eye. It provokes a "new language" as it transforms a political and economic barrier into a positive space of improvisational storytelling. The frontera may be "vague and undetermined" as Gloria Anzaldúa says, but it is nonetheless an historical presence that persists in the stories told by Kumeyaay, Quechan, Cahuilla, and Cocopa, whose lives and voices each day traverse the borderlands of desert and ocean, city and country, Mexico and California. To hear it, we must allow the very mobility that America equates with migrancy—with illegal immigrants and unwanted "vagrants"—to speak. We must hear what Ramón Ames called the *going*.

Native "going" in the Lower Colorado and Baja has always been rooted in the sacred and secular topographies of the landscape. Even in her extremity, Delfina Cuero maintains her faith in the sacred power of the land. At one point in her narrative she relates how an older relative had received his life's calling in a dream involving one of the Imperial Valley's most prominent landforms. In the dream,

> he was awakened by a man in a fireball drawn by two horses and a dog, all golden and shiny. The man told him not to be afraid but to come with him . . . to Signal Mountain near the Colorado River. They flew through the air and then went inside the mountain. It was all golden inside. There were some men there and they told him not to be afraid. They asked him if he was hungry and to go ahead and eat the food there. He was suddenly real hungry but he looked and there were people all skinned and hanging like meat. He said, "no." Then they showed him some piles of gold. Did he want that? He could have all he wanted, and he would always be rich, but he said "no." Then there was a poor old sick woman sitting there full of sores. He wanted her to get well. They asked him if they should kill her to get rid of her and the sores. He said, "no." They said, "Well, would you go over there and put your mouth on her sores three times and spit it out." So he did and her sores went away. They said, "All right, you don't belong here. You go back and start healing everybody." (51-52)

This is the mountain Anza described in 1776. The soldiers had decided they wanted no part of it when it appeared to draw farther away the more they marched toward it. It was bewitched, they said. For Delfina Cuero's uncle, however, Mount Signal was the sacred place where he had been given his life's work.

Other songs of place, also born of silence and mobility, can be heard among the Cahuilla at the valley's northern edge. Paul Apodaca, a folklorist of Navajo and Mexican descent, has recently written a study of the Cahuilla ceremonials of place—called Bird Songs—drawing on more than thirty years of experience as a performer in the tradition. The Bird Songs of the Cahuilla are perhaps the quintessential example of people using art to knit themselves together with their landscape and history. "Songs are said by the singers to be a sequential set of texts that describe a mythic emergence of the 'First people' and their subsequent travels among the birds and animals around their mythic world," Apodaca explains (152).

To this day, the Cahuilla gather each spring at the Lower Colorado's northern boundary to sing the Bird Songs and chant teasing curses at their opponents in *Peon*, a traditional gambling game. At dusk, "Pickup trucks arrive with loads of firewood and . . . Bird Singers who have gone home for dinner begin to show up with folding chairs." The firewood and folding chairs, the onset of the summer, all signal the continued presence of Native storytelling in this land: "The Cahuilla are going to sing Bird Songs all night" (249).

The people no longer know all the words to all the songs or even what all the words mean. But to the Cahuilla (and the Mojave and Kumeyaay who have adopted some of these songs cycles as part of their own traditions) the Bird Songs unite singers and listeners with the "feeling that we have a social connection, a feeling that we're experiencing something that connects us with the past, . . . I'm connected with those people who sang them before, it's not just me. You're plugged into something that's bigger than you" (169).

In precontact times, such song cycles united Cahuilla communities from the San Jacinto Mountains in the north to the Salton Sink in the south. Once a year, the many Cahuilla lineages would gather together to participate in "the ceremonial of origin." For four days, they listened to the creation story as singers from each lineage took turns in singing their parts of the song.

At other times of the year, the Cahuilla sang songs for birth, naming, initiation, first fruits, rain, curing, and funerary rites. These last were comprised of a special "cycle of songs that were heard only at that time" (85). They were sung by a "professional," the *haunik*, who was the lead ceremonial singer of a village. The haunik had to command a "virtuoso's familiarity with all the songs used in each ritual as well as the particular variations that would be applicable for the differing lineages congregated in a village" (119).

These songs cycles were performed in a ceremonial roundhouse, a sacred place "made of willow poles that held thatched walls and roofing." Apodaca describes the inside of this building:

> [There was] a large room with benches along the walls and a second room situated in the center and rear of the *kishamnewet*. This second room was the repository of the sacred bundle, the *mayswut* which was the physical link between the lineages of the village and their mythological origination. The rest of

the house could be used for meetings, ceremonies, or social dances. It was said the house was alive with spirits. (80)

The house and the songs sanctified the surrounding landscape. When Bird Songs were featured, they reminded the assembled Cahuilla of exactly where they came from.

The last Cahuilla haunik was Joe Patencio, who died in 1974. Even he lived too late to ever have an official house to sing in. Yet the tradition lives on. In his study of contemporary Bird Song performances, Paul Apodaca includes the reminiscences of Antonio Siva, Joe Patencio's protégé, who has carried these reverenced songs into the twenty-first century.

Siva was born in 1923 on the Agua Caliente Reservation near Palm Springs. His grandfather came from Collins Valley and was believed to have the power to turn himself into a bear. His mother came from a village on the Salton Sea. Antonio saw Perfecto Segundo, the last great medicine leader of the Cahuilla, dance the last *warrapiat* dance (Apodaca 86). From his mother's family he heard the work songs of the Imperial Valley Cahuilla. As a youth he drifted, working as a migrant laborer in the almond harvest in California's Central Valley. There, hundreds of miles from home, in the migrant labor camps among other Native men, Antonio first heard the Bird Songs. They stayed with him his whole life.

Siva was drafted into the army during World War II and became adept at operating the army's heavy equipment thousands of miles from home. But all the while, there were the songs. He remembers, "I used to sing those Bird Songs while I was operating the cranes and the bulldozers. I kept hearing those songs no matter where I was" (Apodaca 95).

When he got out of the service and returned to California, Siva found the Cahuilla homelands being ravaged by postwar development. Palm Springs had become a haven for movie stars. Almost by accident, he and his sister, Katherine Siva Sauvel, "became identified as advocates for cultural renewal" (Apodaca 64). They urged their fellow Cahuilla to resist development and return to the practice of their traditional ways. To that end, Antonio asked Joe Patencio to teach him the Bird Song tradition, so that the songs of belonging, of how the Cahuilla first came to this land, might give them the strength they needed to resist those who would take that land from them. Although he could never attain the status of haunik—the ceremonial houses were no more, and the elders who once knew the songs of initiation were long gone—he has since become the greatest living expert on the song cycle.

Bird Songs are sung by a group of men who have been trained in the art by an elder. They use rattles, some made of gourds in the traditional way, others fashioned from the detritus of Euro American society—condensed milk cans and the like. While Siva and his group practice traditional Cahuilla singing, these days there are also intertribal groups who perform their own versions of the Bird Songs for mixed audiences of Indian and non-Indian listeners. To outsiders, the words of the songs appear evanescent, even cryptic. "Under the earth a crying sound," one song repeats; another, "Now they are at the edge of the water."

But what sounds simplistic or incomprehensible to the non-Cahuilla listener speaks volumes to the initiated. Apodaca relates how a particularly simple lyric about a woodpecker's call epitomizes the evocative power of these songs to cultural insiders. To non-Cahuilla audiences, "the song simply names the sun and the sounds of the woodpecker and the flicker bird." When Antonio Siva hears it, however, the song embodies the whole sensory experience of morning in the Cahuilla homeland:

> That's the sun is come up and the sun is gone down. This says the sun has come up. It means the sun is hanging, actually. The sun has come up and the woodpecker is singing. The sound of the bird's singing is what the lyric is about and also the flicker bird. The song is about this, it is morning. (Apodaca 154)

His son, Pete remarks, "Americans are so confused by the seemingly few words needed by Indians in their native language communication . . . [but] the Cahuilla speak in word pictures, so that one word conveys a large contextual vision, or reality, to the listener" (Apodaca 167). When one is *of* a place, as these singers and songs are, stories about it bring back the reality of one's experience of that place.

The place names in the songs are equally evocative. "A non-member or person unfamiliar with the Southern California desert," Apodaca reports, would not have the same insight and "might interpret the statements in these lines as generic descriptions of cataclysmic forces instead of specific explanations of still-present land forms" (Apodaca 184). In the Quechan version of the creation story, for example, when Kumastamxo, son of the first creator being, defeats Rattlesnake (Kumaitaveta), the slain monster sprays "blood and spittle in the mountains" along the Colorado, thereby creating precious metals—"the whites call the red 'gold' and the white 'silver'" (Hinton and Watahomigi 481). The nearby Luiseño and Kumeyaay, tribal communities who have adopted Bird Songs into their own traditions, make ground paintings to accompany these melodies, further rooting the songs in the earth where they are sung (Hinton and Watahomigi 198).

Apodaca speculates that the Cahuilla lands in the Imperial and Coachella valleys "may be a terminus in an areal network of languages that extends from Southern California at least as far north as the Western Mono [nation]" (186). He bases his hypothesis on the fact that the songs are sung in words so old that they "predate the current historical groups who learned [them] from an older, now dissipated indigenous structure" (130). Like so many things in Indian country, the songs are "old like hills, like stars." Some of the Cahuilla *tloache* songs (prophetic or divination verse) even use the words of an "'ocean language' which no one understands" (196). Here, in the driest of American desert valleys, the language of the people embodies the cadences of waves lapping the shore of an inland sea that has long since ceased to be.

Over the centuries, Bird Songs have spread along "natural corridors of valleys, deserts, rivers, and coastlines," (20-29) and are now shared by such a diverse set of Native peoples in the Lower Colorado and Coastal Range that Apodaca believes they describe "the evolution of a geographic area of common aesthetic and social organization" (132). Such regions are called "culture areas," and from the evidence provided by the Bird Songs, it appears that the Imperial Valley has been the nexus of story and landforms for thousands of years.

The picture of the Lower Colorado that emerges from the Bird Songs is "conjectural" in the best sense of the word. The songs embody potent gestures. They evoke sounds carried on the desert wind, the glint of a woodpecker feather among spiny chollas, the sheen of standing water on bedrock. Some of the words are just vocables—nonlexical syllables that evoke a mood or subject through timbre rather than semantic meaning—common to many types of American Indian music.

Bird Songs are also sung by the Mohave along the Colorado River at the desert's eastern fringe, and linguistic evidence suggests these too came to the region a long time ago. These song cycles often allude to the specific routes certain families or lineages took on their journey to the homeland. Such routes are related in turn to the most important song cycle of all, the origin story, which was sung communally in precontact times over several days and nights during "an annual ceremonial event wherein the dead of the previous year are memorialized" (Apodaca 178).

To a contemporary Native poet like Georgiana Valoyce-Sanchez, listening to Birds Songs arouses a bittersweet meditation on the delicate balance between tradition and transformation that is Native storytelling in California today: "Down the hill the freeway" [is] "indifferent   mindless / of the bird's song" (*Rattles and Clappers* 81–82). Like Delfina Cuero's autobiographical storytelling practice, the Bird Songs evoke the feeling that there is "more to it" than can be given in an ethnographic report, an outsider's visit.

South and east of the traditional Cahuilla homelands commemorated in the Bird Songs lies the only Indian reservation in the Imperial Valley. Situated on the border with Arizona, at a place on the Colorado River known as the "narrows," is the Quechan Nation. A Yuman-speaking community that has occupied this landscape for several centuries, the Quechan watch over a forty-five-thousand-acre tract of rugged desert peaks, irrigated farmlands, and one casino. The story of the Quechan's tenure in the Lower Colorado is embodied in a complex weave of sacred songs, government reports, and ethnographic questionnaires.

Quechan tradition explains that all Yuman-speaking tribes originally descended from the top of a sacred mountain to the north—Avikame, the Yuman word for Spirit Mountain. Their cultural and linguistic cousins, the Kumeyaay, say that

> if you go there now you will hear all kinds of singing in all languages. If you put your ear to the ground you will hear the sound of dancing. This is caused by the spirits of all the dead people, who go back there when they die and dance just as they do here. That is the place where everything was created first.
>
> —Kumeyaay Nation web site: http://www.kumeyaay.com/history/religion1.html

Some time in the past, perhaps more than a thousand years ago, the Yuman-speaking peoples left the area around Spirit Mountain, fanning out into the Arizona and California deserts. The Quechans of the Lower Colorado took a southern route, led by their culture hero, Marxókuvék, the first Quechan created by Kwikumat, the creator. This trail down the Colorado was called *xam kwatcan* ("another going down"), and the Quechans' tribal name is itself a form of that phrase, *kwatcan* (Forbes 4). At Yuma, Marxókuvék fell ill and the people, with great difficulty, carried him over the river. At Castle Dome (known in Quechan as *Avixolypo*), he told them: "'This is my homeland. Here we shall live. Burn my body by yonder mountain.' Then he died, with his head to the south" (Luthin 487). The trail is still visible, punctuated by petroglyphs and pictographs that mark sacred sites of worship along the way. Present-day Quechan people call this route of pilgrimage the "trail of dreams." It is the record of their "going," made visible in the landforms of the region. Like the Bird Songs of the Cahuilla, the *xam kwatcan* is a migration story writ large on the landscape itself.

Since the day that Marxókuvék was laid to rest, the Quechan sense of community and storytelling has been bound up with this place. Living on the narrows, their lives also became tied to the rhythms of the Colorado River. The people would plant fields of calabasas in the rich silt left by the periodic floods, which in turn watered their crops each year. All of this was watched over by many hills, like Pilot Knob, to which their spiritual leaders repaired each year for visions and ceremonies.

With the coming of the Europeans, however, the landscape along the narrows took on a distinctly colonial cast. The Quechan's life as colonial subjects began in 1776, when the Anza expedition left Father Garces behind to establish a mission among them. By 1781, the Quechan had had enough of their uninvited guests and attacked the Spanish garrison, killing Garces and driving the remaining Spaniards away. According to the missionaries' reckoning, there were about eight hundred Quechan living at the narrows during this period. Like other southwestern tribes, they finally lost most of their autonomy to the U.S. Army in the 1850s. It wasn't until 1883 that the government "finally set aside land on the east side of the Colorado for a reservation for the Quechans" (Bee 19). Unhappy with this arbitrary location, the Quechan requested—and received—permission to settle in encampments on traditional grounds on the California side of the river. They have lived there ever since.

Like many Native communities in the West, the Quechan's reservation was reduced by 80 percent within a few short years of it being granted them (Bee 50). In 1904 Congress passed legislation that "declared all irrigable portions of the Quechan reservation to be public domain," but historian Robert Bee has shown how that agreement "turned out to be a cruel sham." No irrigation canals were even built until 1910 (Bee 67). When they finally *did* build canals, the Reclamation Service charged the Quechan Nation for them. Stripped of their traditional occupations, Quechan men found employment as day laborers with the building of Laguna Dam in 1909, setting the stage for a century-long pattern of off-reservation economic subsistence.

The assault on the Quechan homeland continues to this day. In 2001, the U.S. Department of the Interior announced that it was reversing a ruling made during the Clinton administration and would now consider a bid by Glamis Gold, Ltd., to conduct open-pit mining near Indian Pass, along the *xam kwatcan*. The company's plan calls for three open pits 850 feet deep. Two pits would be filled in after mining, but the third would be left unfilled because the company believes filling it would not be cost-effective.

The Quechan Nation has protested, arguing that "the Quechan Tribe's ability to practice their sacred traditions as a living part of their community life and development would be lost." In a 2002 interview with the *New York Times*, David Hyatt, vice president of investor relations at Glamis Gold, Ltd., commented, "We've offered to move some of our waste stockpiles to accommodate these trails of dreams and whatnot" (Madigan). Hyatt's characterization of Quechan lifeways as "whatnot" is typical of the European practice of silencing Native traditions.

In spite of such ignorance, the Quechan landscape refuses to be silenced, telling its story to whomever will make the effort to walk the *xam kwatcan* and experience its voices. Across the Quechan homeland archaeologists have noted "lithic remains and ceramic scatter" that speak to centuries of human/landform interaction. From Avikame in the north to Castle Dome in the south, hundreds of petroglyphs commemorate those places where Quechan elders have communed with the spirit beings. Archaeologist David Whitley believes much of this rock art depicts "the creation of the world." It is the Genesis of the Yuman-speaking peoples. Yet it tells its story in a unique way. Unlike the European myth, "which implies a sequential narrative depiction of the main occurrences during creation," Whitley explains, "rock art consists of geometric designs and images that are intended to portray the pattern or essence of the creation. Inasmuch as each shaman's version of this myth was different, so too are the . . . patterns unique" (93–94). As the Cahuilla's Bird Songs evoke the landscape rather than describe it, so does the valley's rock art embody the many "shapes" of creation. At each site, a different medicine visionary from Quechan tells a slightly different story.

Even more stunning are the region's geoglyphs—huge animal and human forms and geometric shapes scraped into the ground by clearing lines of dark rock (desert pavement) to expose the lighter soil beneath. One of the most spectacular examples of the storied nature of Native landscape can be found in the Imperial Valley's Yuha Desert, east of Calexico. These gigantic intaglios portray an intricate pattern of geometric designs and the mountain lion, a sacred creature among the Yuman tribes (see figure 26).

Geoglyph sites like this were used in rituals commemorating myths and for purification with ceremonial dances. The layout of the Yuha site suggests that it was used "in group ceremonies, led by shamans, that reenacted the creation of the world. Participants walked along a ritual pathway or circuit, scraped into the desert pavement in the same manner as the geoglyphs, stopping at certain marked spots corresponding to the events described in the myth" (Whitley 95). At places like this throughout the Imperial Valley, especially following the *xam kwatcan* along the banks of the Colorado, Yuman peoples *placed* themselves in a landscape that was itself in direct touch with the first creation. The songs and stories they sang and recited there were their way of telling themselves into presence in this place, among these specific landforms, within this desert's silence.

Not far to the south, across the border in the Mexicali Valley, the Cocopa people who share the Quechan's creation stories still live in hope of the stories' promise of deep presence in the land. Hope Miller, a Cocopa woman who assisted linguist James Crawford in his efforts to create a Cocopa grammar in the late sixties, explained to him the storied nature of this desert landscape that so many Europeans had called "desolate," "bleak," and God-forsaken. "I am all right here," Miller told Crawford, "I am here and own the land with my heart" (Crawford 499).

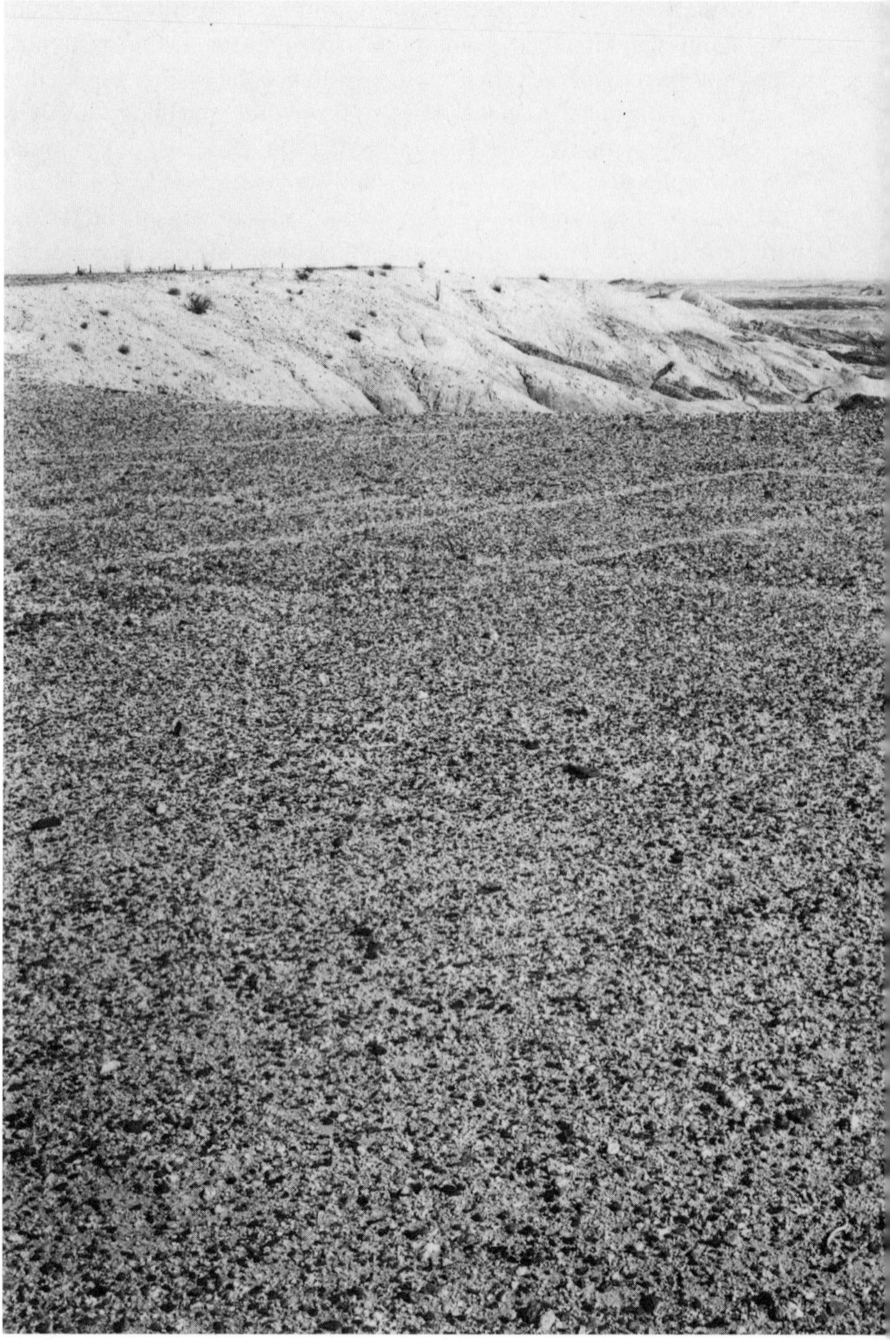

FIGURE 26.
Mark Ruwedel, *Lake Cahuilla, Yuha Desert. The Yuha Geoglyph.* (Reconstructed by Jay Von Werlhof in 1981).
© Mark Ruwedel 1996.

EPILOGUE

"Are there mandolins of western mountains?"

| Anthropologists have called human-made landforms like the Yuha geoglyphs "landscapes of engagement"—a term that conceptualizes place as integrally related to the human societies that inhabit it. "Place and human beings are enmeshed," one rock art researcher notes, "forming a fabric that is particular, concrete and dense" (David 30). That is also a good description of how storytelling has impacted the land and lives of Imperial Valley residents and visitors for more than a thousand years. Photographer Mark Ruwedel took a picture of the Yuha Desert that reflects the crossroads-nature of this place (figure 27). In it, three pre-Columbian Native trails fork outward from a location near the Yuha geoglyph, reflecting the long-standing presence and diversity of human communities across a landscape viewed as uninhabitable by the first Europeans to see it.

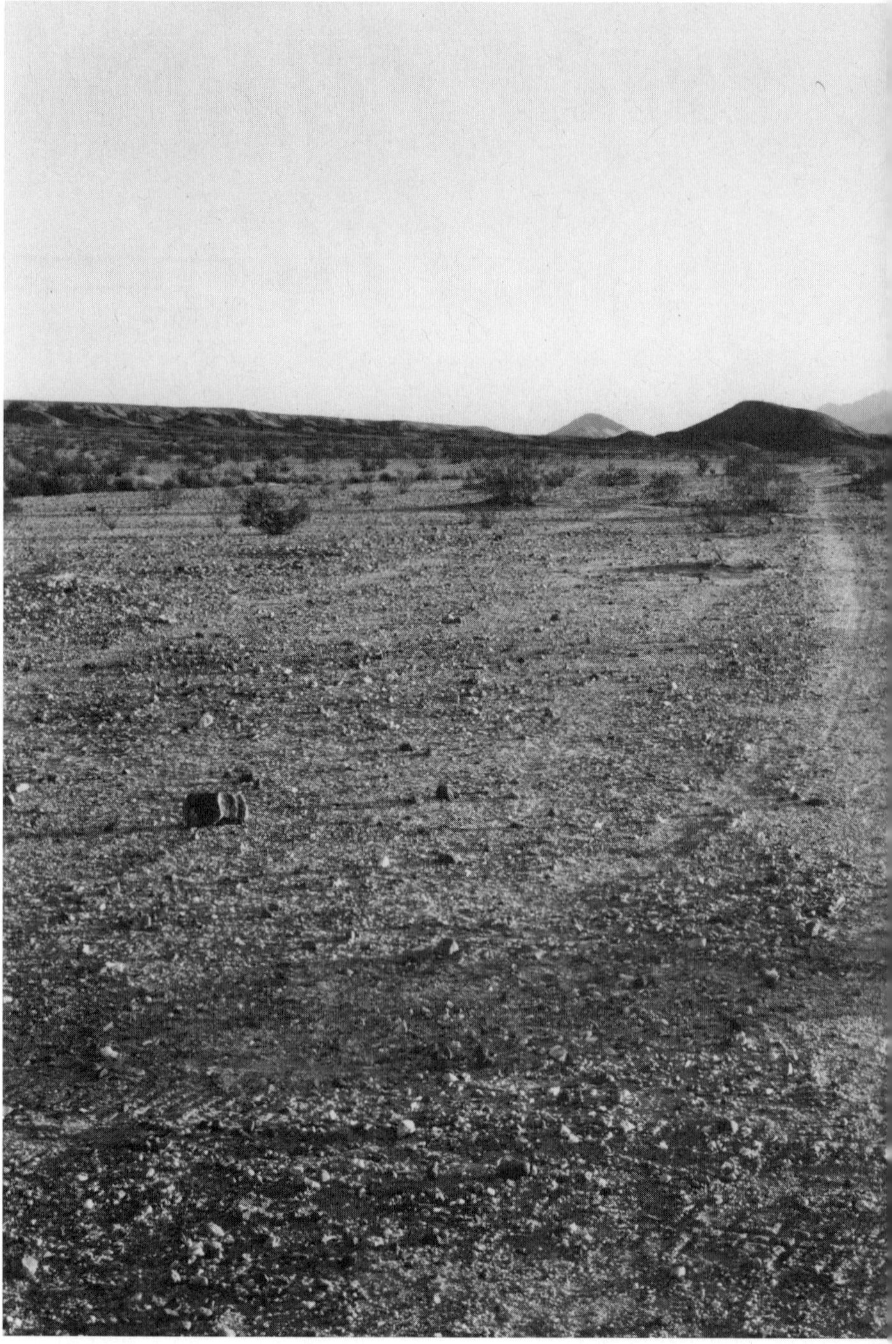

FIGURE 27.
Mark Ruwedel, *Yuha Desert: Where the Ancient Trail Divides into Three.* © Mark Ruwedel 1996.

This book has in a sense imitated those precontact trails, following divergent paths out from the valley's Native, storied center. In the process, I have tried to complicate received notions about storytelling and its high-culture, published counterpart, literary regionalism. Such notions have reduced the relationship between story and place to a dialectic between the cosmopolitan and the local. In contrast, I have worked to allow the reader to hear other resonances and see other configurations. The international border provides the most obvious difference between storytelling here and tales spun in the South or the Midwest, but it is by no means the only one. The historical forces that have shaped both the people and landforms of the valley—immigration, reclamation, the continuing presence of Native peoples in their centuries-old homelands—all make the storytelling here distinct, different even from other desert borderlands in Arizona and New Mexico.

More stories have been told here than can be encompassed in one book. I've had to pass over some landforms whose fascinating histories deserve books of their own—places like the Superstition Mountains of the valley's western fringe, and the northern Chocolate Mountains, which for fifty years have been home to a navy gunnery range. More than once, sitting astride a tractor in the northern part of the valley, I watched the dumb show of streaking fighter bombers attack the treeless, volcanic range, saw dust-cloud evidence of a successful strike, and then mentally counted off the seconds before I heard and felt the rumble of the blast itself.

Some locations in the valley's built environment that received little attention in the pages above also have stories to tell. There is Plaster City, where on any given day a passerby on the Evans Hughes Highway to San Diego will encounter a town dusted in a fine white coating of gypsum, like confectioner's sugar, where the sheetrock mill turns the desert mineral into walls for homes and condos. Not far from there, at the Naval Air Station at Seeley, the navy's Blue Angels practice their aerial acrobatics, crazing the too-blue desert sky with intricate geometric jet trails, rocking the placid winter wheat with raucous sonic booms. At the valley's opposite boundary, there is the town of Felicity, founded in 1986 by Jacques-Andre Istel, a Frenchman who authored *Coe, The Good Dragon*. Recognized by the Imperial County Board of Supervisors as "the center of the world," Istel's town is a bizarre collage of European history and New Age spiritualism. A piece of the Eiffel Tower and a copy of Michelangelo's representation of the finger of God from the Sistine Chapel rise awkwardly out of desert sand near a recently constructed, scaled-down pyramid. Visitors are instructed to make a wish and receive an official certificate documenting their stop at the earth's center.

There are also many more human communities whose valley stories should be told. There are immigrants from South Asia who married into Mexican families in the valley and prospered in this irrigated oasis. These life histories are so vividly dramatized in the documentary film *Roots in the Sand* (1998) that I felt to try write about them here would not do them justice. The stories of the Chinese, Filipino, and Swiss immigrants' valley adaptation also merit telling. One of my high school classmate's father was a former Negro Leaguer who came to the valley in the 1940s. I often wondered what his story was. In spite of these limitations, I hope this book will inspire readers to look at their own homelands with fresh eyes and to tune their ears to its own unique cadences. Every place is, after all, an impossible land in its own way, until the imagination reaches out to the landforms and transforms them into the stuff of storytelling. Human beings everywhere wish to feel a connection to the earth beneath them, to the land on which they live, against which they survive, and through which they share their lives with each other.

Wallace Stevens once said, "The soul is . . . composed / Of the external world" ("Anecdote of Men by the Thousands"). For Stevens, art was the name for the process by which human beings reach out to their physical surroundings and interact with them to create something new, both inside and out. As such, art is life. From this perspective, inscription, storytelling, poetry, painting, dance, and architecture—even the built environments of canal and berm—all become art.

While Stevens tended to think of places made from the soul as entirely imaginary, I have presented the stories of a place, the Imperial Valley, as things that become ever more real over time. Stories woven of the "vocabularies of looking" of different individuals and groups outlive their creators to become traditions; traditions in turn become as tangible as the landforms that hold them in suspension in the human imagination, in a constant conversation between thought and substance. In the Imperial Valley, souls have been composing their external worlds in this way for thousands of years, and even though this book has focused primarily on the published and celebrated examples of this process in the Lower Colorado, there are countless other stories that mark more personal and private engagements with these landforms and people.

Locals tell their children stories of how La Llorona lurks on a dark stretch of country road south of Brawley. The wailing woman, eater of children, waits out there to gobble up kids who disobey their parents or stray too far. A friend of mine heard those stories as a child, and when she and her family had to drive home late along this road, she would tell her daddy to drive faster, to get out of there, so La Llorona wouldn't get them. Even as an adult, the place still gives her a chill.

Nowadays, I teach the story of La Llorona from an American Literature anthology, explaining how the colonial occupation of the Southwest scarred the locals, inspiring them to people their stories of place with images of horror and transfiguration. La Llorona, a new-world Medea, evil twin to the blessed Virgin of Guadalupe, stalked the southwestern night seeking revenge on the colonizers and the children they abandoned as they continued on their way to Cibola, or wherever, their promises of a better life no better than the dust they kicked up as they rode away.

The tales of these people who met the colonizers, whose lives were crossed over and discarded in the wake of "discovery," have now become "texts," where the ruptures and fissures of colonial life splay open the page to an otherworldly play of signifiers. But my friend's story always comes stubbornly back to me as a *fact*, resisting the text I want to make it, and reminding me how place often tethers a story to some landform, bringing it to ground—even a story whose textual life has become woven into a tapestry of colonial conquest and repression. Somewhere, perhaps for my friend's children, the wailing woman still lurks behind the deep night shadows of the salt cedar trees on Dogwood Road, south of town, where the streetlights give way to fields and canals and an abandoned cotton gin.

For others, everyday life in the valley gives rise to song. That is the case for Ramón Becerra, who trekked north from his native Jalisco to seek his fortune in the United States in the 1950s. He was literate in Spanish, and liked to read and write. In the valley, he found work as a tractor driver, which he has been doing ever since. Ramón has taken night classes in Brawley—partly so that he could learn English well enough to become an American citizen and partly to nurture his love of reading and writing. Like most men who stand ten-hour shifts on Caterpillars in eighty-plus-acre parcels throughout the valley, Ramón has plenty of time to think. Between memories of home, lost loves, and the grinding squeal of the Caterpillar's tracks, song lyrics come to him. Sometimes, he writes them down.

Recently, Ramón gathered together money he'd been saving for years and took his songs to a professional recording company in Mexicali. They were recorded by popular Baja Ranchera singer, José Luís Palacios. Titled *Mi Valle Imperial*, the resulting CD speaks of the loneliness of an immigrant laborer far from home, driving his rig sometimes seven days a week in irrigated farmland many miles from the nearest town. The quotidian pleasures of such work—the glimpse of a passing locomotive, the call of a mourning dove, the infinite regress of row crops that on clear days stretch from Mexico to Palm Springs—these make up Ramón Becerra's soul as he goes about composing his external world.

The title track of Becerra's CD offers a homespun encomium to the valley's fertile fields: "En éste valle, se siembran muchas cosas / se siembran mucha talpa, lechuga y algodón" ("In this valley, they plant many things / they plant lots of . . . lettuce, and cotton"). In another lyric passage, Becerra playfully shapes valley town names into passable, danceable quatrains: "Con me paseado por todo sus pueblitos / Por Calipatria y Brawley y de Niland y Imperial" ("In passing through all its small towns / Through Calipatria and Brawley, through Niland and Imperial"). Not high art, perhaps, but vigorously partaking of the several storytelling traditions I've explored in the pages above. Becerra's CD is part developer's dream, part reclamationist celebration, solidly Mexican in its music, its Spanish lyrics, its longing for home. Like the songs of the more famous Los Tigres del Norte, Ramón Becerra's lyrics are "simultaneously national and transnational" and "make space for an alternative narrative" of what contemporary border theorist, José David Saldívar calls "the ethno-racialized cultures of displacement" (3, 7).

Local banker Leonard Vasquez, on the other hand, likes to tell another kind of story. A former rodeo rider, Vasquez is also a published poet, a talespinner in the idiom of cowboy poetry. His coming of age in the valley was marked by the confluence of his skill with a rope and his flair with a pen.

Summers growing up, Leonard "cowboyed it in the feedyards, [and] drove tractors." He went to college, majored in commercial credit banking, and seemed destined for a life as a young professional. Fate intervened, however, when Leonard found himself at loose ends a few months after graduation, waiting for a job offer in banking.

When a friend told him that the Spanish Ranch—the largest cattle operation in Nevada—was hiring, Leonard threw his saddle into the back of his pickup and headed north. That summer was spent out on the range, far from a corporate cubicle, gathering cows and calves, branding them, salting them down, living out of a tent. One day, when it was too rainy to salt down any more animals, too wet to brand, Leonard was stuck in a tent with nothing to do. To while away the time, Leonard wrote. While "some guys are braiding rawhide," Leonard remembers, "I'm over there scratching on a little pad." Across the tent, one eighteen-year-old cowhand whiled away his time looking at *Playboy*. Seeing that Leonard was writing, the kid asked

Leonard to read to him, because he was illiterate. Sitting there, reading articles aloud from *Playboy* magazine and jotting down random thoughts, Leonard became a poet.

When summer ended, he headed back down south to a banking job in the valley. It wasn't until 1985, when the cowboy poetry gathering in Elko was founded and Leonard saw an article about it in the *Brawley News*, that he returned to the notes he'd put down in that tent in Nevada. In 1988, Leonard was awarded a prize buckle at a poetry reading in Prescott, Arizona. Cowboy poetry was suddenly hot: "Guys were getting on the Johnny Carson Show."

One of the most important things Leonard learned about writing came from a cowboy poet who worked at the Four Sixes Ranch. Buster McLowery told Leonard that cowboy poetry was not just about being a good poet. One also had to be a good cowboy. "Our work weeds us out," McLowley said. "If some idiot or honyawker gets up there . . . it's not going to sell, there are people who will sense that." What Leonard learned from McLowery is also central to the stories of place in this book. Their "truths," like the truth of cowboying, comes from "a combination of the things that happen . . . the words, the wording, the equipment that is used, the gear and so forth." Leonard's poems, like all good stories of place, turn on the reader's sense of their authenticity.

But, as the stories of this impossible land also reveal, there isn't one truth to be found in a place, one set of rails that lead to the bottom of the sea. Truth, like the land, is itself "impossible." Social critic Hannah Arendt noticed this many years ago when she tried to sort out a proper response to the Holocaust. In an essay on Arendt's methodology, Lisa Disch, a professor of political science at the University of Minnesota, argues that Arendt's search for an impartial—rather than simply objective—critical understanding of modern political terrorism and oppression lay in the rather humble human practice of storytelling. Professional social scientists ridiculed Arendt's approach for its lack of empirical foundation. Yet the philosopher insisted, Disch explains, that the key lay in "telling oneself the story of an event or situation from the plurality of perspectives that constitute it as a public phenomenon" (666). Only by piecing together all the fragments of human experience of an event—the eyewitness account, the letter from a friend, the piece in the Sunday paper—can one begin to formulate a response that is in turn "on-the-ground" and concrete. Only by witnessing a plurality of such utterances can one begin to shake off the mind-numbing abstractions of modern life that allow us to treat a living landscape as board feet and bushel, and the humans who live and work that land as stereotypes—growers, *braceros*, "non-achievers," cosmopolitans, and locals.

As I said in the opening pages of this book, my story of the Imperial Valley begins with the tale of a train at the bottom of the sea. But it doesn't end there. It has grown to include a flash of a kimono against the desert sand, a novel by Graham Greene, a snapshot of dust-bowl migrants, a stone desert pavement smoothed to form the outline of a mountain lion. If my story has to end for now, I want it to end on a well-traveled stretch of county blacktop near a cinderblock building whose faded sign reads, "Everybody's Market."

I first heard about it from my buddy Frank, who stopped in there for a beer after work one summer evening. From the outside, "Everybody's Market" looked like a hundred other little stores that dot the valley at random corners of its 160-acre sections. They all had ratty screen doors that snapped closed behind you and big jars of pickled eggs and bags of *chicharones* on the counter. The beer was never very cold and the desert cooler on the side wall squeaked like the wheel in a hamster cage.

Frankie stopped in because the store was then new—and on the way—and when he got to the counter he asked why it was called "Everybody's Market." A big Latino guy with a flyswatter sat behind the counter, and Frankie said he acted like he'd been waiting all day for someone to ask him that question. "Well," he says, "I go around town and I see Frank's Market and Joe's Market and Tom's Market, but I think—this is *Everybody's Market*. So I named it that." At least that was his story.

A few years later, my wife found this same story in a novel she was reading. The novel was written long after I had left the valley, long after Frank had related his anecdote. Where, finally, did that story come from?

This book has argued that stories about places like Everybody's Market emerge from an "impossible land"—the landscape of storytelling engagement that grounds the efforts of humans to tell themselves into presence in a particular place at a particular time. Some have argued that regions framed by storytellers exist only in the cosmopolitan fantasies of publishers and readers in America's great urban centers. I believe there *is* something to region, but only if one looks at it from the perspective of relation, from both inside and outside, cosmopolitan and local, in an impossible negotiation between implacably real landforms and deeply personal meanings. "Are there mandolins of western mountains?' Wallace Stevens asked. Does the soul reach out with a particular timbre to meet its surroundings? I believe it does. There *are* mandolins of western mountains and Bird Songs and Norteñas too.

BIBLIOGRAPHY

Ammons, Elizabeth. "The Engineer as Cultural Hero and Willa Cather's First Novel, *Alexander's Bridge*." *American Quarterly* 38, no. 5 (Winter 1986): 746-60.

Anaya, Rudolfo, and Francisco Lomelí, eds. *Aztlán: Essays on the Chicano Homeland*. Albuquerque, NM: Academía/El Norte, 1989.

Andres, Benny Joseph. "Power and Control in the Imperial Valley, California: Nature. Agribusiness, Labor, and Race relations, 1900-1940." Ph.D. diss., University of New Mexico, 2003.

Anzaldúa, Gloria. *Borderlands/La Frontera: The New Mestiza*. San Francisco: Aunt Lute, 1987.

Apodaca, Paul. "Tradition, Myth, and Performance of Cahuilla Bird Songs." Ph.D. diss. UCLA, 1999.

Appadurai, Arjun. "Place and Voice in Anthropological Theory." *Cultural Anthropology* 3, no. 1 (February 1988): 16-20.

Audubon, John W. *Audubon's Western Journal: 1849-1850*. Cleveland: Arthur H. Clark, 1906.

Austin, Mary. *The Land of Little Rain*. 1903. Reprint, New York: Penguin, 1988.

Ayers, Edward L., Patricia Nelson Limerick, Stephen Nissenbaum, and Peter S. Onuf, eds. *All Over the Map: Rethinking American Regions*. Baltimore: The Johns Hopkins University Press, 1996.

Basso, Keith H., and Steven Feld, eds. *Senses of Place*. Santa Fe, NM: School of American Research Press, 1996.

Bean, Lowell John. "Cahuilla." In *Handbook of North American Indians*, vol. 8, ed. Robert Heizer. Washington, DC: Smithsonian Institution Press, 1978. 575–87.

———. *Mukat's People: The Cahuilla Indians of Southern California*. Berkeley: University of California Press, 1972.

Bee, Robert L. *Crosscurrents Along the Colorado: The Impact of Government Policy on the Quechan Indians*. Tucson: University of Arizona Press, 1981.

Bezner, Lili Corbus. *Photography and Politics in America: From the New Deal into the Cold War*. Baltimore: The Johns Hopkins University Press, 1999.

Brodhead, Richard. *Cultures of Letters: Scenes of Reading and Writing in Nineteenth-Century America*. Chicago: University of Chicago Press, 1993.

Brown, Zoe. "Dorothea Lange: Field Notes and Photographs, 1935–1940." Master's Thesis, JFK University, 1979.

Browne, John Ross. *Adventures in the Apache Country: Tour through Arizona and Sonora with Notes on the Silver Regions of Nevada*. 1871. Reprint, New York: Promontory Press, 1974.

Crary, Jonathan. *Techniques of the Observer: On Vision and Modernity in the Nineteenth Century*. Cambridge: Harvard University Press, 1992.

Crawford, James W. *Cocopa Texts*. University of California Publications in Linguistics, vol. 100. Berkeley: University of California Press, 1983.

Cuero, Delfina. *Delfina Cuero: Her Autobiography*. Ed. Florence Shipek. Banning, CA: Ballena Press, 1991.

Daniel, Cletus. *Bitter Harvest: A History of California Farmworkers, 1870–1941*. Berkeley: University of California Press, 1981.

Dasenbrock, Reed Way. "Southwest of What? Southwestern Literature as a Form of Frontier Literature." In *Desert, Garden, Margin, Range: Literature on the American Frontier*, ed. Eric Heyne. New York: Twayne, 1992. 123–32.

David, Bruno. *Landscapes, Rock-art, and the Dreaming: An Archaeology of Preunderstanding*. New York: Leicester University Press, 2002.

Davis, Mike. *City of Quartz*. New York: Vintage, 1992.

DeBuys, William Eno. *Salt Dreams: Land and Water in Low-down California*. Albuquerque: University of New Mexico Press, 1999.

Disch, Lisa J. "More Truth than Fact: Storytelling as Critical Understanding in the Writings of Hannah Arendt." *Political Theory* 21, no 4 (November 1995): 665–94.

Dixon, Maynard. *The Drawings of Maynard Dixon*. San Francisco: Achenbach Foundation for Graphic Arts, Fine Arts Museums of San Francisco, 1985.

Dozier, Deborah, ed. *The Heart Is Fire: The World of the Cahuilla Indians of Southern California*. Los Angeles: Hedey Press, 1998.

Entrikin, Nicolas. *The Betweenness of Place: Towards a Geography of Modernity*. Baltimore: The Johns Hopkins University Press, 1991.

Forbes, Jack D. *Warriors of the Colorado: The Yumas of the Quechan Nation and their Neighbors*. Norman: University of Oklahoma Press, 1965.

Galarza, Ernest. *Strangers in Our Fields*. Washington, DC: Joint U.S.-Mexico Trade Union Committee, 1956.

Gifford, E. W. *The Kamia of Imperial Valley*. Smithsonian Institution Bureau of American Ethnology, Bulletin 97. Washington, D.C.: Smithsonian Institution, 1931.

Gupta, Akhil, and James Ferguson, eds. *Culture, Power, and Place: Explorations in Critical Anthropology*. Durham, NC: Duke University Press, 1997.

Gutiérrez, Ramón A. "Nationalism and Literary Production: The Hispanic and Chicano Experiences." In *Recovering the U. S. Hispanic Literary Heritage*. Houston: Arte Público Press, 1993. 1:241–50.

Haas, Lisbeth. *Conquests and Historical Identities in California, 1769–1936*. Berkeley: University of California Press, 1995.

Hansen, Arthur A., and Betty E. Mitson, eds. *Voices Long Silent: An Oral Inquiry into the Japanese American Evacuation*. Japanese American Project: Oral History Program. Fullerton: California State University, Fullerton, 1974.

Harris, Elizabeth, ed. *Imperial Valley's First Three Families and the Church They Founded*. Imperial, CA: Imperial County Historical Society, 1997.

Hayes, Alfred S. "Field Procedures while Working with the Diegueno." *International Journal of American Linguistics* 20, no. 30 (1954): 185–94.

Hinton, Leanne, and Lucille J. Watahomigie, eds. *Spirit Mountain: An Anthology of Yuman Story and Song*. Sun Tracks: An American Indian Literary Series, vol. 25. Tucson: University of Arizona Press, 1984.

Hirsch, Eric, and Michael O'Hanlon, eds. *The Anthropology of Landscape: Perspectives on Place and Space*. New York: Oxford University Press, 1995.

Hosokawa, Bill, and Robert A. Wilson. *East to America: A History of the Japanese in the United States*. New York: William Morrow, 1980.

Howe, Edgar F., and Wilbur J. Hall. *The Story of the First Decade in Imperial Valley, California*. Imperial, CA: Edgar F. Howe and Sons, 1910.

Jackson, Helen Hunt. *Ramona*. 1883. Reprint, New York: Penguin, 1988.

Imperial County Health Department. *Imperial Valley Border Health Initiative*. Imperial, CA: 1999.

Jordán, Fernando. *El Otro Mexico: Biografía de Baja California*. 1956. Reprint, Mexico: Secretaría de Educación Pública, Frontera, 1976.

Karem, Jeff. *The Romance of Authenticity: The Cultural Politics of Regional and Ethnic Literatures*. Richmond: University of Virginia Press, 2004.

Kikumura, Akemi. *Through Harsh Winters: The Life of a Japanese Immigrant Woman.* Novato, CA: Chandler and Sharp, 1981.

Lange, Dorothea. Ms Field Notebook (June 1935). Dorothea Lange Collection, Oakland Museum of California.

Lange, Dorothea, and Paul Schuster Taylor. *American Exodus: A Record of Human Erosion.* 1941. Reprint, Paris: Jean Michel Place, 1999.

Lears, T. Jackson. *No Place of Grace: Antimodernism and the Transformation of American Culture.* New York: Pantheon Books, 1981.

Levy, Jacques E. *César Chávez: Autobiography of La Causa.* New York: Norton, 1975.

Limerick, Patricia Nelson. *Desert Passages: Encounters with the American Deserts.* Albuquerque: University of New Mexico Press, 1985.

Lucero, Hector Manuel. "Peopling Baja California." In *Postborder City: Cultural Spaces of Bajalta California.* London: Routledge, 2003. 83–115.

Luomala, Katherine. "Tipai and Ipai." In *Handbook of North American Indians*, vol. 8, ed. Robert Heizer. Smithsonian Institution Press: Washington, DC, 1978. 592–609.

Luthin, Herbert W., ed. *Surviving through the Days: Translations of California Stories and Songs: A California Indian Reader.* Berkeley: University of California Press, 2002.

Lutz, Tom. *Cosmopolitan Vistas: American Cosmopolitanism and Literary Value.* Ithaca, NY: Cornell University Press, 2004.

Madigan, Nick. "Tribe Prepares for Renewed Fight over Gold Mine." *The New York Times* (January 7, 2002).

Manje, Juan Mateo. *Luz de Tierra Incógnita: Unknown Arizona and Sonora, 1693–1701.* Ed. Harry J. Karns. Tucson: Arizona Silhouettes, 1954.

Matsuoka, Jack. *Camp II, Block 211: Daily Life in an Internment Camp.* San Francisco: Japan Publications, 1974.

Meltzer, Milton. *Dorothea Lange: A Photographer's Life.* 1978. Reprint, Syracuse, NY: University of Syracuse Press, 2000.

Momaday, N. Scott. *The Man Made of Words: Essays, Stories, Passages.* New York: St. Martin's, 1997.

Patencio, Francisco. *Stories and Legends of the Palm Springs Indians.* Ed. Margaret Boynton. Palm Springs, CA: Palm Springs Desert Museum, 1943.

Raeburn, John. *A Startling Revolution: A Cultural History of Thirties Photography.* Urbana: University of Illinois Press, 2006.

Reisner, Marc. *Cadillac Desert: The American West and Its Disappearing Water.* New York: Penguin, 1993.

Rogers, Will. *Will Rogers' Weekly Articles.* Ed. Steven Gragert, vol. 4. Norman: Oklahoma State University Press, 1981.

Ruwedel, Mark. *Written on the Land.* Vancouver, Canada: Presentation Gallery, 2002.

Saldívar, José David. *Border Matters: Remapping American Cultural Studies.* Berkeley: University of California Press, 1997.

Sarasohn, Eileen Sunada. *The Issei: Portrait of a Pioneer, an Oral History.* Palo Alto, CA: Pacific Books, 1983.

Sarris, Greg, ed. *The Sound of Rattles and Clappers: A Collection of New California Indian Writing.* Sun Tracks: An American Indian Literary Series, vol. 26. Tucson: University of Arizona Press, 1994.

Silva, Simón. *Small-Town Browny: Cosecha de la Vida.* San Bernardino, CA: Arte Cachanilla, 1998.

Smythe, William. *The Conquest of Arid America.* 1905. Reprint, Seattle: University of Washington, 1969.

Stone, Connie L. *The Linear Oasis: Managing Cultural Resources along the Lower Colorado River.* Cultural Resources Series No. 6. Washington, DC: BLM, 1991.

Tagg, Lawrence V. *Harold Bell Wright: Storyteller to America.* Tucson: Westernlore Press, 1986.

Teague, David W. *The Southwest in American Literature and Art: The Rise of a Desert Aesthetic.* Tucson: University of Arizona Press, 1997.

Tout, Otis B. *The First Thirty Years in Imperial Valley California.* 1931. Reprint, Imperial, CA: Imperial County Historical Society, 1990.

Trujillo Muñoz, Gabriel. *El Festín de los Cuervos.* Bogotá, Columbia: Grupo Editorial Norma, 2002.

———. *Mexicali: Un Siglo de Vida Artistica y Cultural, 1903–2003.* Mexicali, Mexico: Fondo Editorial de Baja California, 2003.

Uchida, Yoshiko. *Desert Exile: The Uprooting of a Japanese American Family.* Seattle: University of Washington Press, 1982.

Valdés, Gina. *Puentes y Fronteras /Bridges and Borders.* Tempe, AZ: Bilingual Press, 1996.

Van Dyke, John C. *The Desert.* New York: Scribner's, 1901.

Veitch, Jonathan. *American Superrealism: Nathanel West and the Politics of Representation in the 1930s.* Madison: University of Wisconsin Press, 1997.

Villarreal, José Antonio. *Pocho.* 1959. Reprint, New York: Anchor Books, 1989.

Villaseñor, Victor. *Rain of Gold.* Houston, TX: Arte Publico Press, 1991.

Wharton, Edith. *The House of Mirth.* New York: Charles Scribner's Sons, 1969.

White, Richard, and John M. Findlay, eds. *Power and Place in the North American West*. Seattle: Center for the Study of the Pacific Northwest in Association with the University of Washington Press, 1999.

Whitley, David S. *The Art of the Shaman: Rock Art of California*. Provo: University of Utah Press, 2000.

Wild, Peter, ed. *The Autobiography of John C. Van Dyke*. Provo: University of Utah Press, 1993.

Wild, Peter C., and Neil Carmony. "The Trip Not Taken..." *Journal of Arizona History* (Spring 1993): 65-80.

Work Projects Administration. *The Story of Japanese Farming in California*. Prepared under the direction of Emil T. H. Bunje. Berkeley, CA: WPA, 1957.

Wright, Harold Bell. *The Winning of Barbara Worth*. Chicago: Book Supply Company, 1911.

Yamauchi, Wakako. *Songs My Mother Taught Me*. Ed. and with an introduction by Garrett Hongo. New York: The Feminist Press, 1994.

INDEX

Abbey, Edward, 50
American Exodus (Taylor and Lange), 70–71, 73, 75, 77, 84, 91, 103
Ames, Ramón, 159–61
Ammons, Elizabeth, 57
Anaya, Rudolfo, 135
Andrade, Guillermo, 54
Andres, Benny Joseph, 72
And the Soul Shall Dance (Yamauchi), 125–27
Anza, Juan Bautista de, 16, 21, 23, 24, 28, 39, 132, 152, 167
Anzaldúa, Gloria, 13, 130, 160
Apodaca, Paul, 161, 162, 164, 165
Arendt, Hannah, 180
Audubon, John W., 24
Austin, Mary, 12, 50
Avikame (Spirit Mountain), 152, 166, 168
Ayer, Edward L., 50
Aztlán, 135–36

Barbara Worth Hotel, 65, 68, 72, 144
Bajacaliforniense, 141
bajalta, la, 139, 141
Baker, Ray Stannard, 10
Becerra, Ramón, 178–79; *Mi Valle Imperial*, 178
Bee, Robert L., 167

Big Bowl, 38, 45, 47, 50, 52, 53, 152. *See also* Salton Basin; Salton Sea; Salton Trough
Bird Songs, 161–66, 168, 181
Blue Angels, 176
Bracero Program, 140
Brawley, 85, 90, 129, 130–32, 133, 136, 177, 178, 179
Brodhead, Richard, 8
Browne, John Ross, 24

Cahuilla, 23–24, 151–53, 161–66
Calexico, 25, 28, 118, 139, 147, 168
California Development Company (CDC), 54–56, 60
Calipatria, 29, 72, 179
Calling of Dan Matthews, The (Wright), 57
Cantu, Ernesto, 139, 141, 147
Carmony, Neil, 33
Cather, Willa, 8
Chaffey, George, 25, 28, 55–56, 61
Chávez, César, 129–31, 136
Cocopa, 61, 152–53, 160, 169
Colorado River, 4, 19, 21, 25, 34, 37, 38, 44, 45, 52, 53, 58, 61, 117–18, 139, 154, 161, 165, 166, 167
Colorado River Land Company (CRLC), 139, 141, 153
Common Sense, 69

| 189

Crary, Jonathan, 46
Crawford, James W., 169
Cuero, Delfina, 153–61, 166

Daniel, Cletus, 71
Darwin, Charles, 38
Dasenbrock, Reed Way, 12
Díaz, Porfirio, 139, 141
Disch, Lisa J., 180
Dixon, Maynard, 73–74

ejido, 140
El Centro, 28, 65, 118, 133, 147

Farm Security Administration (FSA), 75–76
Festín de los Cuervos, El (Trujillo), 144
Forbes, Robert H., 152
Fox, Vicente, 146
Fremont, John C., 10
Fuji, Toshita, 107

Garcés, Father, 152, 155, 167
Garland, Hamlin, 8
Genthe, Arnold, 73
Gentleman's Agreement, 108–9
Glamis Gold, Ltd., 180–81
Goldwyn, Samuel, 52, 58–59, 64
Greeley, Horace, 9
Greene, Graham, 148, 181

Heber, Anthony, 54–55, 57
Holt, W. F., 56–57, 65
Holtville, 97
Hongo, Garrett, 106

Hudson River School, 33, 37, 43

Imperial, 28
Imperial Irrigation District (IID), 28
Istel, Jacques-Andre, 176
Ives, Joseph, 24

Jackson, Helen Hunt, 11
Japanese Internment, 117–22
Jefferson, Thomas, 6
Jordan, Fernando, 140, 144

Kazin, Alfred, 70
Kearney, Stephen W., 23
Kono, Junhei, 112
Kumeyaay (Tipai), 23–24, 151–60, 162, 164, 166

Lake Cahuilla, 21–22, 44
Lange, Dorothea, 69–103
Lawless Roads, The (Greene), 148
Lears, T. Jackson, 64
Llorona, La, 177–78
Lomelí, Francisco, 135
Lower Colorado Desert, 15–25, 28, 34, 44, 46, 50, 53, 75, 122, 124, 125, 127, 129, 136, 145, 151, 161, 165–67, 177
Lummis, Charles, 11

Maeda, Robert, 118
Matsuoka, Jack, 118–19
Meloland, 68
Mesquite Road (Trujillo), 144
mestizaje, 134

Mexicali, 25, 28, 105, 130, 136, 138–41, 144–60, 169, 178
Miller, Hope (Cocopa), 169
Mi Valle Imperial (Becerra), 178
Mojave (Indians), 162
Mojave Desert, 33, 35, 38
Momaday, N. Scott, 15, 153
Mount Signal, (Signal Mountain), 16, 65, 161
Movimiento, El, 135

Naguchi, Isamu, 118
Niland, 179
Noh Plays, 126–27

Ota, Mildred, 118

Palacios, José Luis, 170
Patencio, Francisco, 152
Patencio, Joe, 163
Perigrenaje, La, 130, 133, 136
Perry, Charles N., 65
picture brides, 108
place: anthropology of place, 13–14; Frontier Hypothesis, 34; genius loci, 18; landscapes of engagement, 173; New Western History, 13–14; regionalism, 6–9, 13, 73, 147, 176
Plaster City, 176
Pocho (Villareal), 131–32, 135
pocho, 132, 135–36
Poston, AZ, 117–22

Quechan (Yuma), 22–24, 152–53, 160–69
Quivira Society, 12

Rain of Gold (Villaseñor), 136
Rogers, Will, 72
Roosevelt, Franklin, 117
Roosevelt, Theodore, 37, 57
Roots in the Sand (Jayasri Majumdar Hart), 177
Ruwedel, Mark, 173

Salton Basin, 21, 28, 38, 44, 52, 53, 57, 62, 106, 152. *See also* Big Bowl; Salton Sea; Salton Trough
Salton Sea, 1, 22, 28, 30, 31, 138, 163. *See also* Big Bowl; Salton Basin; Salton Trough
Salton Trough, 21–22, 153. *See also* Big Bowl; Salton Basin; Salton Sea
Sanchez, Georgiana, 153, 165
Sauvel, Katherine Siva, 163
S̶e̶e̶l̶e̶y̶, 176
Shepard of the Hills, The (Wright), 51, 56
Shima, George, 108
Shipek, 155, 159
Silva, Simón, 136–38
Siva, Antonio, 163–64
Small Town Browny (Silva), 136–37
Smith, Yvonne, 68
Smythe William, 11
Stevens, Wallace, 6, 177, 181
storytelling: 1–4, 9, 13, 130, 153, 160, 173–81
Stryker, Roy, 75, 91

Tagg, Lawrence V., 56
Tanaka, Michiko, 111

| 191

Taylor, Paul Schuster, 70, 74–76, 84–85, 91, 96
Teague, David W., 10
That Printer of Udell's (Wright), 56
Todd, Charles, 69
Tout, Otis B., 65, 68
Trujillo, Gabriel Muñoz, 140–41, 144–45, 147, 149; *Festín de los Cuervos*, 144; *Mesquite Road*, 144
Turner, Frederick Jackson, 34
Twain, Mark, 6

Uchida, Yoshiko, 118, 120–21, 125

Van Dyke, John C., 31, 33–50, 52–53, 74, 123, 125, 152–53
Vasquez, Leonard, 179–80
Villarreal, José Antonio, 112, 135–37, 144; *Pocho*, 131–32, 135
Villaseñor, Victor, 136–37; 144; *Rain of Gold*, 136
Volstead Act, 139

Wharton, 33, 35
White, Richard, 13
Whitley, David S., 168
Wild, Peter C., 33
Winning of Barbara Worth, The (Wright), 11, 52, 57–59, 63, 68, 70–72, 110
Wright, Harold Bell, 11, 29, 51–52, 54–65, 68–71, 76, 110; *Calling of Dan Matthews*, 57; *Shepard of the Hills*, 51, 56; *That Printer of Udell's*, 56; *Winning of Barbara Worth*, 11, 52, 57–59, 63, 68, 70–72, 110

Yamauchi, Wakako, 103, 106–7, 109–13, 116–18, 121–27; *And the Soul Shall Dance*, 125–27
Yuha Desert, 22, 168, 173
Yuha geoglyph, 168
Yuha Man, 22